Publish and be damned
www.pabd.com

The SELF Service Universe

by
Sheridan King

Publish and be damned
www.pabd.com

First published in Canada 2006 by Sheridan King.
The moral right of Sheridan King to be identified as the author of this work has
been asserted.

Designed in Toronto, Canada by Adlibbed ltd.
Printed and bound by Lightningsource in the US or the UK.

ISBN:1-897312-29-6

Publish and be Damned helps writers publish their books. Our
service uses a series of automated tools to design and print your book
on-demand, eliminating the need for large print runs and inventory
costs. Now, there's nothing stopping you getting your book into print
quickly and easily.

**For more information or to visit our book store please visit us at
www.pabd.com**

For:
Jane, Sonia, Elizabeth,
baby TJ, Mother & Father,
Sue for her love,
Steve & Sarah,
'Raven Lady', Milena,
Prof, Lui Krieg,
Tim Wheater & Natalie, Francesca,
Jelle, Maddie & Bella,
His Holiness The Dalai Lama:
may Tibet be free.

INTRODUCTION
The simple secret of success in life is an unshakeable determination not to fail. Wandering Star

Hello there and welcome to the SELF Service Universe! I am here to share with you the powerful and timely message that *you can change your life.* You can improve your circumstances, health, wealth and happiness. Whatever dreams you have can become a reality when you understand, and use, the amazing wish-fulfilling power of the Law of Attraction in this SELF Service Universe. This book will help you gain that understanding and show you how to use this law to get what you really want.

So, what is it that you really want right now? Do you know the answer? If you do, why do you keep getting all sorts of other things and circumstances that you don't want instead? Of course if you don't know what you want that's already one good reason why you haven't already got it! Either way, I think we can both agree that you could use a little friendly help right now.

I am here to help you understand that whatever you can imagine you can attract into your life by infallible law. This law has been known and understood for thousands of years. It is only just becoming known today because for so long it has been concealed, deliberately kept secret by the few who had most of the wealth, power and glory. But the time has come for the truth to be made known to all.

Let us understand that there IS enough of everything to go around in this abundant universe. It is not a shortage or lack of good things and circumstances that keep you and most of humanity from getting what you want. It is a lack of knowledge and experience of how *the Law of Attraction* operates.

To be more specific it is a lack of knowledge about how your own thoughts, beliefs and actions influence the results you get from the law of attraction.

Through the Law of Attraction the SELF Service Universe exists to grant your wishes and respond to your commands. Nothing is impossible for the universe when it is acting on your command. You can literally help yourself to anything you want, to your heart's desires. That is why I call it the SELF Service Universe.

The method is very simple. You *decide* what you want, *ask* for it, *believe* that it is yours already and then *receive* it when the universe delivers. It doesn't need a book, not even a page to write the method down.

However as we know simple doesn't necessarily mean easy. In fact most of you who seek out this book do so because what you usually get seems to be what you don't want. You can at least take some comfort in realising that are not alone. At *least* 95 percent of your fellow humans alive today are in the same situation.

Why? If the SELF Service Universe (SSU) is at your command how come it keeps delivering stress, bills, troubles and the things you don't want? If you can help yourself to anything the universe can create for you, why do you keep coming away with stuff you don't want?

Together we will explore these vital questions and come up with meaningful answers. THAT is the purpose of this book.

It is going to take your time and commitment for a little while but what do you have to lose? Nothing! In fact you have everything to gain and someday you will look at the modest price you paid for this book as one of the wisest, most powerful investments you have ever made.

The key to getting you what you want from the SELF Service Universe, free express delivery included, is for you to make a shift in your awareness and to stop undoing your wishes with negative thinking, beliefs and lack of focus. To make a change in your life's circumstances, your current reality, you must first change your thinking. You are going to need help and guidance in this task. That is a role I have happily accepted and I have worked very hard to put this book together just for you, right here, right now.

So do you want to stop getting what you don't want in life? Do you want to start getting what you do want?

Good then ASK for it, right now. This IS the key in the ignition waiting to be turned to start the engine that will take you where you need to go.

Just ASK how to stop getting what you don't want and start getting what you do want.

Your wish is your universe's command!
Let us begin.

Sheridan King
November 2006
West Yorkshire, England.

THIS IS WHERE IT BEGINS
Do not fear going forward slowly, fear only to stand still. Chinese Wisdom

You are living in a physical and spiritual universe, which you, like most people, know very little about. That's not to say that many minds haven't turned their attention to attempting to unravel its secrets. So far there have been some fascinating insights and many theories but there's a long way to go. That's understandable because as far as we can tell the universe has been around for a very, very long time and, to be frank, human scientists haven't. So whatever they have already discovered and whatever theories they come up with it's all quite an achievement for the new kids on the block.

But there's a part of every one of us that is as old as the universe itself. The scientists can back me up on this because it's known the atoms and elements of our physical forms are billions of years old. That's known and understood. From 'Big Bang' to the present every elementary particle has been on a journey. It just so happens that the journey finds many of them in this part of the universe and in our bodies. Long after our bodies have gone, those atoms will still be travelling. That's an amazing thought. If you are wearing a gold ring at this moment you are wearing something made from an element that was originally forged in the heart of an exploding star!

But I want to focus on another aspect of the universe that isn't exactly physical and so easily measurable by science. It is what is behind the existence of these eternal atoms and all matter in the universe. I am looking at that spiritual and eternal energy field that underpins and supports the physical version. We'll be looking at this as we move through this book but for now I just want you to enjoy reading and exploring the concepts and teachings in this little book of mine that you are holding.

I am so happy that you are reading this because I wrote this book for YOU. I wrote it to share with you the keys to the incredible power you have to create and master your own destiny! In gaining your personal power and achieving SELF Service, you can also help others to improve their lives and circumstances if you wish. Whether you are going solo or you want to share this adventure with those you love is entirely your choice.

My job is to help you to understand your potential, to show you how to make a difference to your life and become a happier and more successful member of the human race. In the truest sense you can gain control of your life and destiny. However good or bad you feel your life is, you can make changes for the better. By getting hold of this book you have already taken the first step on the journey to understanding the infallible Law of Attraction, your true nature and the magic of the SELF Service Universe.

When I first began to create this book I was somewhat ahead of my time. You see I did a lot of work for this book well over a decade ago. That was long before the current fashion for anything to do with what is now being called "Cosmic Ordering" or the "Law of Attraction".

Everywhere I go now (I'm editing this in late 2006 by the way) I see books and programmes such as "Cosmic Ordering" by Barbel Mohr, "The Cosmic Ordering Guide" by Stephen Richards, "Cosmic Ordering; How to make your dreams come true" by popular Sun-sign Astrologer Jonathan Cainer, and even "Positively Happy" by British television personality Noel Edmonds all coming out on the subject. This isn't a race or a competition so I am very happy to give their books this publicity right here in my book.

You see I don't have to operate from a limiting negative belief of 'lack'. There are enough points of view and enough people in the world who need some help and guidance to make many more such publications possible and in fact necessary. These are all useful tools for someone who has an open mind and wants to begin making their life better.

There has also been an explosion of people promoting two particularly impressive and fascinating DVD films lately. One is called "What the Bleep do we know?" and it is a mind-stretching tour-de-force of our universe and the implications of quantum research. It features thought provoking ideas and interviews with leading figures from various fields of research including philosophy, psychology, quantum physics and theology. It is worth watching because what scientists are researching and discussing clearly points to a universe and reality that is more like a mind than a machine.

The other film is the incredible and memorable presentation of the long concealed and suppressed secret of the Law of Attraction. Not surprisingly the film is called "The Secret". This is a life-changing programme that introduces us to the simple, powerful but long concealed and suppressed secret of our own power to create our lives and circumstances. It features the ideas of many interesting people including the Joe Vitale and the amazing Life Success Mentor, Bob Proctor. I give you more information about this at the back of this book.

I think these are all great tools for those who want to make changes to their lives. I recommend them to you as well worth your attention. But there's still the need to explain how and why people are not attracting what they *want* from life. Why they are not consciously making use of the Law of Attraction. Or why, without some necessary understanding and support, they probably won't be too successful if they do.

There are so many people in the world who are regularly 'cosmically ordering' from the SELF Service Universe, whether they know it or not, but they are not in control of the process. That is why they keep throwing up their hands in despair as yet more stress, financial pressure, and unpleasant circumstances piles into their lives. They, and you, need some HELP and need it now.

Some of the books touch briefly on this matter but for many people who are up to their necks in things and circumstances they don't want that is simply not enough. I decided that there was a real need for a detailed explanation of what is really going on and influencing the outcomes. This means that I have to make sure the Law of Attraction and how it operates in the SELF Service Universe is fully understood. But equally vital and more involved is the requirement to help you to understand your true nature, To dispel the myths and illusions that hide you from your true, limitless SELF that is intimately connected to all things in this SELF Servcie Universe. I want to explain to you how you operate consciously and subconsciously, to show you how to reduce or eliminate the negative habits and processes that work against you. You need this help and this book is the guide to show you how to get free and use your maximum potential.

In order to change your circumstances you have to change yourself. None of the teachers and success coaches working around the world today will deny this. Changing your thinking sounds simple but it not easy to do. Most people do not have the knowledge and tools necessary to accomplish it. You see those few and rare happy folks who are truly benefiting from the Law of Attraction and featured in (or actually writing) those other books, have already done something about their hidden negative habits. They have done some necessary work on themselves to maximise their ability to use the potential of the SELF Service Universe. That work on liberating the true power and nature of your SELF has been the core of my teaching for many years.

In my role as spiritual coach and executive mentor I have worked with people from all walks of life, of all ages, creeds and backgrounds. My job has always been to help them explore and discover themselves and develop strategies to optimise their success and happiness, whether privately or in their business lives. For many the process has introduced them to their true nature and the Spiritually Existing Love Form (SELF) that is the eternal aspect of their being and intimately connected to the true power of the universe.

The fact that their lives were constantly challenging them with circumstances that they didn't want was a key motivator for them. I know that everyone got positive results in proportion to the effort and commitment they made to do the work on themselves. The teaching helped them to understand who and what they were as players in this physical universe. It helped them see how they and they alone were responsible for all the unwanted and unpleasant things and circumstances that kept coming around in their lives. The teaching showed how their subconscious negative thinking, beliefs and programming constantly undermined their positive wishing.

You have this book because you are seeking to improve your life and circumstances. Your SELF knows this and has created the situation that has brought you and the book together in the same place. Now it is probable that most of the work was done subconsciously but the good news is that you placed your order with the SELF Service Universe and it delivered. That's the power you have and can really develop to transform your life.

Actually my whole life is living testament to that power we all possess. I understood and used it from being a very small boy. I remember a story of how a journalist asked Mahatma Ghandi for his story. The great and peaceful leader replied by simply stating to the journalist that his life *was* his story. My story is my life so far, and it has been an amazing and crazy journey.

I have always known that anything was possible and I could do anything if I really decided to. As a small child I became a violinist and took to it straight away. My violin teacher, Herbert Marriner, was the father of famous concert violinist and conductor Sir Neville Marriner. I truly loved 'pop' Marriner and his wife and they became my honorary grandparents when my own grandparents died. Pop entered me in many Music Festivals and every one I entered I won.

I also admired an inspiring music teacher at School. His name was Stuart Wilson and he was a crazy and exciting pianist, conductor and mentor to yours truly. What a great example he was of the power teachers everywhere have to empower the young!

At the age of 16 I won a scholarship to a school of music and was taught by a talented and warm-hearted man called Herbert Whone. He was tall, slender, and played the violin like an angel. The very first time we met he and I had a connection that made us feel like we had always known each other. Have you ever had that feeling when you've met someone? To me, with my love and interest in Tibet, the Himalayas and spiritual masters he was a true yogi! During my time at music school I decided that I wanted to be an Opera Singer too. I did exactly that scoring very highly in my practical exams. Right from an early age my annual holiday with my family was at Butlins. It soon became my ambition to be a Butlin Redcoat but I would have to be 18 years old before I could do the job. I was told that redcoats were 'one in a million". Many applied but only a few were ever selected. Well you can guess the rest. On my 18th birthday I stood on stage in my new uniform as a new redcoat entertainer.

I decided to become a stage magician and produced my own stage shows for children. I became a regular visitor to magic conventions and even performed magic tricks for listeners over the airwaves as a local radio personality. There are still a few tricks up my sleeve to this very day!

My life has carried on that way and I have to say having a mother who was clearly on the same wavelength as her son didn't do me any harm either. Nothing surprises my mother Marie about what I do. If I called her in Mallorca where she lives and told her I'd decided to become Prime Minister or perhaps an astronaut she'd be pleased and supportive. You see she shares my confidence and has absolutely no doubt about my ability to do anything that I put my mind to.

There's a great and empowering lesson in this. The greatest gift any parent can give to their children is to do what my mother did; always support your child's dreams and always tell them that they have the potential to be anything, and do anything, that they choose. As a parent I have not always been exactly wildly ecstatic about some of the choices my daughters have made but I have always supported them and been ready to assist them if necessary.

You should always put your effort and energies into living your own dreams. But it is also a good thing to encourage and allow others to live theirs. It is sad to see how some people's 'happiness' depends on dismissing other people's dreams or living their dreams through someone else. Everyone should have dreams and be given every encouragement to make them become a reality. I love it when someone's dream comes true. That's the SELF Service Universe's delivery service doing a great job for someone who earned it.

Since leaving school and college I've had plenty of dreams and ambitions and I always will. A goal or a horizon isn't the ending, the fence around our lives and our potential. To me a horizon is something I want to get to because, once I'm there, there are bound to be new horizons I didn't see before. So through the SELF that is my true being and via the services of the SELF Service Universe, I continue to dream and make it so.

Over the years I have been a radio broadcaster, a cabaret artist, professional magician and children's entertainer. I am also an inventor (with patents to prove it), an award winning graphic designer, a well-known wristwatch collector, award winning sales trainer, e-commerce guru, and company director of several companies. I also have a good track record as a success coach and mentor, army officer, public speaker, writer, healer, counsellor, husband, father of two amazing girls (Sonia and Elizabeth) and grandfather of baby 'TJ'!

One client recently asked if he could see my CV. After he'd read it he sat back and exclaimed, "my god man, how old are you? It would take several lifetimes to do all this!" Well if you didn't know what I know I guess it would. But the great thing about knowledge is that it doesn't get weaker or lose its power the more you use it or share it.

Now my life hasn't been all sunlight and pleasure. I have had my troubles, despairs and trials too so you can put aside any idea that I am unusually lucky or immune to life's darker side. Over a period of just a few years I had to undergo four nasty lower back operations, each requiring several weeks of daily out-patient care. I had surgery that left me with a large hole at the base of my spine that had to be packed and unpacked every day for months until my body grew enough new tissue to fill it out. I endured this long, painful process and the routine assault on my privacy and sense of dignity (you try dropping your pants and baring your backside very day to male and female nurses) not once, not twice but four times.

I am so grateful to report that the last operation was a long time ago. I know that this is because I sat down with my marvellous surgeon and asked him to explain in exact detail, how and why the problem (Pilo Nidal Sinus) kept coming back. He did, in nauseating detail! But that was the key. I was able to understand that this was a genetic fault encoded in my DNA down there and then to visualise in my mental Holodeck (more on visualisation later) what processes were involved in this problem. I then sent the command out to the SELF Service Universe to get the Law of Attraction to assist my bodymind to re-pattern my DNA. Well I know that works! That is the true power of the SELF and its relationship with the SELF Service Universe. It is not a secret any longer either!

I am happy to tell anyone about anything that I know. If I know something that has given me advantages, that has made me a 'winner', I am not in least bit worried about sharing it. If I know it and you could do with knowing it too, that's great. Come on down and get it.

I have simple principle about how I relate to my clients, friends and also to complete strangers. It is the principle that we are all connected and can all teach each other something. I want to help you to win. I want you to feel the same way about helping me win too. If I help you win and you help me win we both have a greater chance of being winners! Losers usually occur when one side has a greater desire to win for themselves than they do for the other's victory. So I like sharing and I want you to take what I have learned from this little book and become one of life's winners.

I will share something else very personal with you right now. I have a goal. It's a big, exciting and wonderful goal. I will be an internationally famous life success mentor who is loved, respected and remembered by many people in all walks of life as 'the one' who unconditionally gave them the tools that set them free.

That's the goal I want to achieve, so I guess I will. Will the order clerk at the SELF Service Universe please take note!

CAUSE AND EFFECT CAUSES EFFECTS!

If I were to choose one sentence to sum up my whole philosophy, I should say: allow no evil in your thoughts. Confucius

So I've shared with you the briefest glimpse of how my life has always demonstrated to me that the SELF Service Universe is real and has unlimited potential. So now we need to turn to you and see how we can get you helping yourself to the good things and eliminate the bad. At least that is the effect I think we are both looking for. You are reading this paragraph in this little book right NOW because of a chain of cause and effect that runs backwards through the all the days of your life and beyond. What you do, or do not do, with this book from here on also continues a chain of cause and effect onwards into what we, in our limited human perception, call the future.

One day in that future you will or will not achieve something really massive and important to you and guess what? Yes, you will be able to follow the cause and effect backward to a point where you either took your power, unlimited potential and freedom or you did not. That point can be here and NOW if you so choose.

How do you choose? It is simple, you make a decision to admit that you don't know certain things and that is why your life hasn't yet delivered to you everything that you had hoped and wanted. In deciding this you need to have an open mind to allow me, through these pages, to help you to learn what you need to know.

Everything you have ever experienced in this life, and ever will experience, unfolds under the impersonal universal law of cause and effect. For instance you know that the current effect of reading these words had its cause in you opening the book to reveal this page. If you didn't open the book then this little exchange between us would not be taking place! It's that simple and you will think it is pretty obvious but until now had you really taken responsibility for what was going on in your life by accepting your previous actions as direct cause for the consequences? You have been ready to take the credit for causing the good things but have you come to terms with your part in causing the bad? You have been wishing positively but thinking negatively, mostly without realising it.

18

Please understand that the simple law of cause and effect, also called karma, is automatic and impersonal. It doesn't care or discriminate between a potentially great and good cause and a dark, destructive one. Whatever you set in motion will proceed and deliver its effects without any regard for your personal preferences or comfort! The karmic flow is consistent and those who understand the ground rules can decide to act with mindfulness (more on this later) and thus begin to increase the positive effects and diminish the negative ones. You improve your outcomes in life by acting with awareness at all times.

Sadly there is no get-out clause in this 4D universe so you need to accept that cause and effect never stops and never stands still. Neither will it give you a free ride and let you coast for a while. No, every tiny instant of the now you must be moving ahead and reaping the results of the actions, the causes, that have taken place. So you need to understand that doing nothing doesn't get you off the hook either. Inaction is, in terms of universal law of cause and effect, just as potent as any action.

As time flows the effect of this law is to either create or to disintegrate the path towards anything you want. The really important thing is to use this knowledge and decide what causes and eventual effects you want to create in order to get the life you want. Equally you need to learn the strategies that will help you to avoid disintegrating the progress. You want to be able to empower the realisation of your dreams. You need to be sure that whatever you are doing is *moving you towards the attainment of a desired outcome.* Remember that if you are not moving towards what you want you are moving away from it.

Just by picking up this book instead of doing something else you have already changed your life and your future. How incredibly powerful every action can be in your life! Of course everyone else also has that same power. The sad thing is just how many of them don't know or realise that they, and they alone, hold the key to their future and the realisation of all their dreams and ambitions.

I see so many people who are not happy. They know they are not living the lives they want. There are so many of them out there who are seeking the answers you now hold. Sadly all these seekers are under the impression that the power to change their lives for the better is to be found, at some expense, in obtaining the necessary 'lucky charm', submitting to some guru or external authority, through consulting psychics, mediums and so on.

They also often believe that their unhappiness is entirely caused by someone or something other than themselves. That's like searching a house for something you know that you lost in the car!

It saddens me to see all these dissatisfied people, particularly when I attend the various mind, body, spirit events, looking everywhere for a 'magic key' to unlock their limitations and make them happy. They look all around and eagerly seek this magic key in so many locations, never seeing it is always wherever they are. You see the magic key, the mystical wish granting jewel, is right *there*. It is within you always. It cannot possibly be anywhere else! I am so grateful for every opportunity I have to help a person realise that everything they need to create the life they want is within them. It always has been inside awaiting their commands and it is never going to be found anywhere else.

But you are different because you already know this and somewhere you set a chain of events in motion that has brought this teaching to you. So now you have the edge, the advantage, and can start to understand why so much of what you have had in life was not what you wanted. Right now you have the opportunity to explore your power and I am simply here to help you. Together we'll investigate your true nature and locate the magic key within. Only you can turn the key and unlock the unlimited potentials of your SELF and the SELF Service Universe. But that's okay after all, you don't mind doing a little work for such a vast reward do you?

I am really excited to have been given this opportunity to tell you that you ARE the key. That you, and only you, truly are the greatest source of power for changing your life. You don't need to look for it anywhere else, climb mountains, and dig holes or anything other than look within. It is SO close, that magic key, and yet if you look for it outside it will be forever out of reach.

Getting aware of the key is entirely down to you and by understanding and co-operating with your power you can really have whatever you want in your life. You can achieve anything you really choose to set as your goal and the only thing that can ever stand in your way is you. I know because I am living proof of what SELF-power can do. Nothing and no one can stand in my way and keep me from my goals once I unleash my personal power and invoke the SELF Service Universe. Neither can anyone or anything stop you if you so choose. That's right, you are your most powerful tool for getting what you want.

Of course there are two sides to everything in this 4D universe of ours so it follows that you can also be your most powerful opponent. The great news is that we can, together, explore and understand how to become your own champion and avoid frustrating and derailing your dreams. You can have the life you want but you have to go and get it. More importantly you have to intend it and attract it to you by the infallible law that has already been acting upon your every action and command since the day you became a thinking, feeling member of the human race. I am going to explain this to you as we go along but I will do so in a way that best serves you in understanding and then putting into practice the methods for becoming a free and self-determined being.

That will require you to have an open mind and to choose to really think about what I have to tell you. Let's be clear about this. I am putting before you the fundamental secrets of who and what you truly are and also what you have become. This knowledge will empower you to undo the things that have kept you from realising and using your true nature. It's a process that sets the true you free.

This knowledge of the true nature of human existence has been in the keeping of human teachers for thousands of years. Actually it's been around for more millennia than you and many of your fellow humans might appreciate. I can tell you, and I will later, some simple and incredibly powerful wisdom that has been passed down from generation to generation of mankind for some 50,000 years. Considering the errors and assumptions made concerning even the most recent few thousand years of human history that makes this truly ancient wisdom worth our attention.

Much of what I have to tell you has been suppressed or has been carefully hidden and so you will not have been exposed to it before. It is no accident that throughout human history the most power, the greatest wealth and the greatest freedom has always been held by the few. Those few have been the ones who were well aware of what many other modern teachers and I have discovered. However, the few are not so happy about

21

this knowledge being used by others. They are not really too worried though because this 'new age' is so full of false answers and distractions that so many will see this truth and then wander off.

So this process of getting you to the point that you can command your destiny will need you to pay attention and not get distracted because it seems to good and far too simple to be true. Those who have kept this wisdom for themselves are actually relying on you to do just that. To stay the distance and unleash the power for yourself you must be ready and willing to consider new ideas and you will have to think.

I am not being unkind when I say that a lot of what people consider to be thinking actually isn't. A lot of what passes for thinking is simply the passive soaking up of information, the activation of memory, running on automatic responses, or imagination running freely. If you watch a lot of television, for example, you are not likely to be thinking while you are watching. If you were really thinking you'd miss what was going on in the plot. Instead you are open and the images and sounds come straight in through your eyes and ears and bypass any critical thought processes and analysis.

By the way, I also think a great deal of modern conversation is carried out though habit rather than by thinking. It is usually an exchange of words conducted by stimulus and response using memory and automatic language processing. If you don't believe me then just listen to other people's conversations for a while without actually allowing yourself to become involved and you will begin to see how so much is repetition and standard responses. Clearly a lot of what they are saying shows that they are not thinking! If people were truly saying what they were thinking they'd either be speechless or falling out with each other! Often people will 'dry up' in mid-sentence having clearly lost their place in the conversation. That couldn't happen if they were really thinking.

If you are a driver you will no doubt have the experience of finding yourself at a certain point in the journey and you cannot remember getting there! Goodness me, could it be that you had been driving without thinking? Well yes it could, you were obviously lost in memory, or the radio, or daydreaming and so the automated processes that a moment ago you thought were 'thinking' have taken you quite safely to your destination.

What this process of getting control of your incredible creative power demands, is that you exercise your consciousness. You are bound up in an intimate thought-based relationship with the universe. Your thoughts, and your feelings, are continually radiating out and attracting results whether good or bad. So awareness is vital when are placing orders with the SSU.

You must practice being aware and here now, present fully in each moment, with your conscious thought at your disposal. I am offering you the key to the kingdom of your own best and greatest life and all I ask in return is that you work hard at being here now on this journey. This is another important part of the teaching so stay with me.

I spend a lot of time out amongst you and so many of you are not actually present, actually here in the <u>now</u>. I can be in a crowd and yet, in space and time I am almost alone because everyone else's bodymind is dwelling in something that has already happened, is dreaming about something that hasn't happened yet, or is simply idling. In other words, there's lots of people about but very few of them are present.

I hope you understand the difference because it really is a vital part of getting to the magic key within you. As we move along you'll discover how to exercise your awareness and witness how you think and what your self-talk is about. When you do you'll see what I have been talking about. Because you will realise that so much of your bodymind's mental activity, its thoughts and images, is aimed at things that have already happened or things that haven't yet happened but you think they will. To stop getting what you don't want and begin attracting what you do want you have to learn to be present right here in the now, because only here and now can you consciously command the SELF Service Universe and your true SELF.

I was recently in a meeting with a successful company director. He wanted to know why I managed to create such an impact when I was in the room. It wasn't how I was dressed or even particularly what I did or said that explained the powerful effect I had on him and his colleagues. So I told him. I said that the secret was simple; when I am in the room I am <u>in</u> the room. He was a smart guy and he understood that someone who has 'presence' has it because they are, unlike most people, actually present! The simple act of being truly present gives me the power to make a difference because the present, the now, IS the only place any of us can ever act and invoke the full effects of universal law. We will be taking this simple concept very seriously throughout this book and this journey together.

I need to just explain a little about how I have put this book together because it is structured a little differently to most books. Firstly that is because I am using a teaching technique that uses a 'circular' pattern of recurring elements to help imprint the key learning points in your consciousness. This is an ancient teaching method that means certain phrases and ideas come around more than once in the book. So if you begin to get a sense of déjà vu that's absolutely fine, because the ideas have been passed by your attention before.

I have also taken the unusual step of allocating pages throughout the book for your own use. I have given them the heading "Notes, Ideas and Scribbles" which should give you a good idea of what they are for! I encourage you to make notes in this book and treat it as a valuable tool and a record of your own thoughts and ideas.

I also strongly recommend that you buy yourself a nice notebook that can become your private journal and 'feel good folio'. I will come back to this later but keeping notes of your progress and recording your thoughts and feelings is a useful tool. You should also cut out pictures and articles that inspire you and stick them in your 'feel good folio'. But in any case with the help of those nice people at PABD (the publisher) I have given you space in this book to make notes. Where I thought a little nudge was helpful I have added a quick note about how you might structure your notes, ideas and scribbles. This is your book so use it as you choose and don't be afraid to write in it as the mood takes you!

You will also find that I have placed what are clearly stories between some of the teaching chapters. These stories are an ancient technique of instruction and they introduce a range of concepts and principles for your consideration. They also act as natural breaks in the process this book is using to help you gain insight and understanding that can set you free. The stories are structured as a contrast to the rest of the book and cause you to change mental gears and utilise different parts of your brain and mental faculties. As you come across them relax and enjoy them as a break from the harder stuff!

So, just to remind you of the key points so far:
- You can place an order with the SELF Service Universe for anything you want.
- To place an order decide what you want, ask for it, believe it yours already, receive it!
- You can change your life by changing your thinking.
- When you change yourself your circumstances will change too.
- The universe is more of a mind than a machine and quantum physics is detecting this.
- You are really an eternal SELF, that is a Spiritually Existing Love Form.
- You are in an intimate thought based relationship with the universe.
- Everything unfolds by the laws of cause and effect (karma).
- YOU are ultimately responsible for the circumstances, the effects, in your life
- There is no "time out" from cause and effect.
- Even doing nothing is a cause that will have an effect.
- It is no good looking around for the key to YOUR best life. It is within you – always.
- If you are not moving towards what you want, you are moving away from it.
- Your greatest opponent in getting what you want is your own negative programming.
- Think!
- The only time and place to be if you want to get a better life is here, NOW!
- Get yourself a notebook and keep a journal and 'feel good folio'.

A WAY THAT WORKS

I have three treasures that I guard and cherish: the first is love, the second is contentment, the third is humility. Only the loving are courageous, only the contented are magnanimous, only the humble are capable of command. Lao-Tse

It had its beginnings many years ago in the teaching of friends who who had been seeking a way to make sense of their lives and to discover their true nature and purpose. Many had, like you, realised that life wasn't going quite the way they had hoped. They wanted better things for themselves and needed to find the way to do so. For some students the motive was a genuine and heartfelt desire to become of service to others and to make a difference in the world. For some of the seekers I worked with the motive was a deep sense that things weren't how they were 'meant' to be. It also has to be said that there were also those who simply wanted to 'belong' to something or some cause, in order to feel good about themselves.

My role to these seekers was to be their life coach or spiritual mentor. We met regularly over the years in groups and one-on-one, to look at all the issues arising in their lives.

I was utilising empowerment and guidance techniques that came to me as though I had always known them. Of course, in the realest sense, I *had* always known them. I was living proof that we can overcome our programming, our legacy and be free to make of our lives whatever we choose. I was asked by some of the students if I could record the methods and explanations that I was using so they had a handy reminder when I wasn't around. That is how the first few printed pages of guidance and methods came to exist.

Then along came the phenomenal "lift off" of everything "New Age" that quickly revealed the possibility of a wider audience who might be seekers of what this 'way' had to offer. So the task became one of putting the various notes, recordings and concepts of the training into some form I could publish. Naturally I was aware that this choice to publish was not going to be an easy task, but there again that's usually the way for anything truly worthwhile. I committed time and effort to revising the material and writing any new text where necessary. I admit to some relief when I had finished it!

The end result is now here before you. The way we say things often differs from how we would write them down! But my speaking style and pace seems to transcribe fairly well and I have done my best to strike a balance between grammatical correctness and stylistic impact. Any remaining errors are therefore entirely down to me but do not reduce the power of this work!

I also transcribed some of this book straight from my true, eternal SELF (Spiritually Existing Love Form). Don't worry, I will explain the nature of SELF in detail later as it is a very important subject that has a direct impact on you getting the life you want. So a lot of the material in this book came from my SELF through my fingers and into the word processor as if I was speaking to an audience.

However flawed the work may be from a literary point of view it has one strong redeeming factor – the process herein described *works*. It is a small but powerful book that can make a huge difference to those who make use of the knowledge and techniques to get the life they want. However it is received, it was written with love and compassion for those who need what it contains. I draw confidence from many students, clients and friends who are the living proof of the power of this way.

So this little powerhouse of a book is about empowering you to get what you want rather than continuing to get what you don't want. It is about getting to grips with your true nature and gaining a perspective of your role and place in the universe. It is also about taking steps to increase your vital force and to become master of your personal power. I want to help you to maximise your wellness so you can live a great life the way you want to live it. If you think wellness is a strange word to crop up at this point, just hold that thought because I will deal with this important issue very shortly. It will make sense I can assure you!

This is a book about a process that takes you from where you are to where you want to be. More importantly, it helps you know and understand more about who and what you are, which differs from who and what you currently *think* you are. This process has the potential for those who make the effort to begin obtaining real wellness, freedom and responsibility for their own life and all that it brings their way, good and bad. You will not just gain the knowledge and techniques to make the Law of Attraction in the SELF Service Universe your ally, you will also gain great insight into your true nature and the meaning of life. That sounds like a good offer to me but it is up to you to decide and to do the work.

From a simplistic point of view I can say that life often hurts, and you'll probably agree with me. But life can just deliver pain and suffering or, if you have done the work, it can deliver pain and suffering that has *meaning and purpose.* Surprisingly, whether life just hurts, or hurts with a meaning is actually your choice – even if you are making it subconsciously for a whole range of reasons.

The process explained and explored in this book will help you to understand the power of your thoughts and choices. Learning and applying that which I will show you will give your life experiences meaning and help point out the underlying purpose. In fact the methods and information in this book can do so much more. They provide a route to getting what you want from life, the universe and all therein. That's a great place to be whether you have a desire to be of service to other sentient beings or just simply want to make sense of life.

There is absolutely nothing wrong with taking what this book has to offer for the sole purpose of sorting out your own life and improving your circumstances and personal power. In fact that's a pretty good idea! Whichever way you choose to approach this book you will be embarking on the adventure of travelling through inner space in search of who and what you really are. It is a process of becoming free from the programmes, illusions and damaging limitations written into your operating software (the mind) by your upbringing, education, religion, politics and many other overt and covert influences. It is an explanation of the basic nature of your manifestation as a living breathing physical life form in a quantum universe that is experienced through three physical dimensions (3D) and one temporal dimension (time). I will refer to this dimensional aspect often in the shorthand of '4D'.

It is a voyage, an adventure and sometimes a nightmare too, but I assure you that the results make it well worth staying on course! I will also make recommendations of the works of other authors I feel can expand upon certain points. I have studied the books listed at the end of this work and recommend them to you as interesting and stimulating research.

I will take this opportunity to point out something: I am NOT a person who insists my way is the ONLY one and must be followed and accepted blindly. My way is simply a̲ way that works. So by making suggestions for further study I am exposing you to views and explanations that may reinforce my opinion but can also give other equally valid interpretations. You should absorb what is useful to you, test it experientially, intellectually and spiritually and discard that which doesn't serve on the voyage to becoming free.

A good student and true friend once remarked that this process was *"like the peeling of an onion. Layer after layer is revealed and there's always the possibility of tears!"* I liked that image and it has stayed with me. My friend also wisely observed that the remaining layers often seemed to be infinite in number. What a wonderful reality to get to play in! However long you live you always have the possibility of new experiences and knowledge.

To that true friend, to you who now hold this book and to all my human sisters and brothers everywhere I offer this work for consideration. It is not the only way. It is simply another way that works. I offer it freely and with love.

THE SELF SERVICE UNIVERSE
The spirit that endows all things with life is Love. Tschu-Li

A lot of this book comes directly from my SELF (Spiritually Existing Love Form). In "New Age" terms this might be called "channelling" but whatever label you apply is fine. It's more a case of an internal communications link with my multi-dimensional true form, which is manifesting a small and limited part of itself in this 4D environment. The "I" that speaks here in this physical form is a limited 4D aspect of my SELF that is extruded from the multi-dimensional quantum field of the universe.

I am not a body that has an energy field; I am an energy field that has a body. The same is true of you.

My energy field here in the 4D is an extension from my true SELF. This SELF is existing within the all-encompassing quantum field that science is beginning to get to grips with. This zero point field is a sea of data in a quantum foam that is responsible for every 'thing' that manifests physically in any dimension from sub-atomic particles right up in scale to entire galactic clusters and our universe. My 'soul', my SELF, and that of every sentient being that has ever lived are eternally preserved and consciously existing in that field.

I know that information about this field has been part of human awareness for millennia. In the distant past it was known as "The Hall of Records". I have also heard it referred to as "the Akashic Record". To the Aboriginal peoples in Australia it is "the Dreamtime" and thanks to George Lucas and his "Star Wars" films millions of us also know of it, even if we think it is science fiction, as "the Force".

You can also apply many various religious labels to the supreme or absolute consciousness, that organises and holds all of the zero point field together. Whatever label, cultural or theological perspective is being applied you need to be aware of it and that it is the multi-dimensional sea of consciousness and limitless creative possibilities that is the true source of all existence.

As a SELF (Spiritually Existing Love Form) manifesting into the 4D universe you currently have a physical body, a vehicle, crafted from physical matter but it is really a dance of indestructible, eternal quantum energy.

Every single living breathing person on this incredible planet of ours is the 4D visible tip of a universal iceberg of eternal consciousness (the SELF) and unlimited multi-dimensional potential. Not one human that ever existed was truly ever born or ever died. No, that would be like saying that every time we scrapped a car we were also killing the driver wherever they happened to be!

Now we are only a short way into this little book and yet how's that for fabulously good news? I am telling you that you are a Spiritually Existing Love Form playing at being a 4D Human. The implications are profound: *You are much, much more than you may have ever realised. You are an energy field that's eternal and unlimited in potential and you have eternity and infinity as your playground to get the things, knowledge, wisdom and experiences you desire.*

I hope that makes you feel better already!

What I have just told you is a largely forgotten 'secret' this book has to bring for your consideration. Whatever you paid for this book, this one secret alone makes it the best investment you've made. Go back and read it again, as many times as you like and work on accepting this truth because it is the truth that will set you free. The wisdom, the knowledge, has been known and preserved by a few masters in every generation throughout all human existence and it's incredibly ancient. Perhaps this time of booming business relating to matters of mind, body and spirit shouldn't be called "new age" at all. With truth this ancient it should be called the 'not-at-all new age' instead.

The second secret that this book has to share within you is that the nature of the quantum field, the universal energy field, *is to extrude into the physical 4D realm, to manifest, everything from its pre-existing 'potential' in response to focussed thought.* In other words the universe responds and manifests in response to thought. We will give simple fact this a lot of attention as we go along.

Today the effect of the 'observer' on how the measurements within any experiment in quantum physics unfold is now well known. Quantum physics indicates that all fundamental particles observed 'choose' to manifest in specific space-time co-ordinates from a huge field of 'possible' locations when they collapse their wave function. In fact all particles are, in effect, 'probable' particles until a measurement collapses their wave function and gives them location, charge and spin. That is how the story is unfolding so far. Much of this 'understanding' of the quantum universe will develop over time, as does all human knowledge in response to curiousity, theory and experimentation. But I am only offering this snippet of the science because it appears to be leading in a direction that resonates with ancient knowledge and my own 'knowing' that, through the true nature of the universe, thoughts become things.

We'll get back to this later but just remember that everything is energy. Things are energy and so are thoughts. The nature of the universe is such that *thoughts become things*. As a sentient being dwelling in the 4D manifestation of the SELF Service Universe, you should know the universe is here to assist and support you. Your most dominant thoughts and intentions are energy and they imprint themselves upon the fabric of the SELF Service Universe and become things or circumstances. As an energy field with a body you are creating the things and circumstances in your life, whether you want them or not, by impersonal and impartial law.

You have been told that you are an energy field that animates a body in this 4D realm. In support of this you can easily find plenty of information telling you, and showing you, that your body has an energy field, often also called an aura. There's also plenty of information that talks about other, smaller and separate energy fields within the aura called 'chakras'. The important difference between all this information and the secret I have revealed hangs on looking at the concept of cause and effect used within these other works.

The commonly used explanations regarding human auras and chakras or other subtle energies such as Chi state that the living body causes (creates) the energies as a result of being 'alive' and then emits them, which is the effect.

What I want you to understand is that my SELF tells me it's the other way around. Turning something around by one hundred and eighty degrees and taking another look is a useful tactic. I recommend that you always keep in mind the simple fact that you can always look at anything from another point of view. You can always do what I call a 'one-eighty' on any situation or circumstance. If you make a habit of this you'll find that problems are often opportunities in disguise.

So looking at this idea that a living body causes an energy field from the other way around opens a great possibility. The possibility is that you ARE the primal energy field that happens to incorporate an aura, utilises chakras and you also happen to have a body. The body is said to cause the energy fields but the energy fields from the multi-dimensional quantum field cause the body that then understandably emits the energy in the 4D. You are not a body with an energy field. You are an energy field with a body.

Now someone is eventually going to point out that I am wrong because tests show the aura and chakras are there in a living body but are absent in the case of a dead body. They are simply missing the point and not following the chain of interdependent reality – the sequence of causes and effects – far enough back. The animating cause, the multi-dimensional driver of that physical vehicle, animated it and its functions in life. The energy fields that sustained the driver and powered the atomic, molecular, cellular and organic processes instigated energy production at many levels and frequencies that are measurable in the 4D realm. When the driver, the causal energy field of the SELF withdrew, for whatever reason, the body died and naturally these processes began to run down and stop. So the very case the doubter makes for their point of view sustains the integrity of mine.

You as a conscious energy field have a body, which, whilst you are in residence, appears to have an energy field. We have to be careful when dealing with the 4D and human scale aspect of our existence because most of what we perceive and experience isn't as it 'appears' when you change scale to take a closer look or approach from other dimensions. The one non-physical dimension we inhabit is expressed as time. But we all know that time is relative. Two minutes in a dentist's chair with the drill whistling away can be a lot longer than ten minutes of intimacy with an exciting lover!

The simplicity of being an energy field that has a body rather than being a body that has an energy field is the key to understanding the eternal nature of your true self. The scientific fact that energy is eternal, always preserved, cannot be destroyed but can change its state also provides a useful handle for this whole concept. Knowing the prime cause for your existence is energy that is indestructible, always preserved, beyond the

4D limitations of time, space, life and death but can change its state, is the foundation stone of this teaching. You will build a superior life upon this unshakeable foundation through the processes we will explore together. If necessary go back over the previous explanation again and again until you have it clearly understood. As we will discover later, the possibility of cleaning up the communications channel from 4D to that other, vast and eternal energy field of our SELF, while still residing in this 4D vehicle and universe, is vital if we are going to plot and command our own course through life.

I am grateful to have known all through my current physical life in this 4D realm that there was more to me than this physical body and that I am here for a purpose. Be aware that your body is not an accident of primeval goo and evolution but the intelligent 4D effect of a vast and eternal cause. Your body is superbly designed vehicle and was selected for a purpose.

Knowing, as I do, that there is a good reason for my being here and that I have chosen this particular 'life' for a specific mission really gets me through those inevitable trials and troubles of 4D life! I knew what I was doing when I accepted the mission and I know what I will be doing when it is over, there's no reason I can think of to say that you can't have that same experience. Without this knowledge so much of your existence quite simply doesn't make much sense.

Get used to the idea that you have a wonderful, marvellous vehicle designed and evolved over many generations of human existence. If you take care and drive it well it will get you wherever you choose to go. Service it regularly. Go and get a wellness check and have your tyres kicked, oil changed and your engine tuned! You are an eternal spirit-based consciousness that has chosen to explore the possibilities and growth potentials of this physical universe. So get out the handbook and start learning to be an advanced driver!

Points to consider:
- Everything in the universe is energy. That is a fact. Things and thoughts are energy.
- The SELF Service Universe is a limitless energy field of possibilities.

- The SSU has unlimited potential to respond to YOUR dominant thoughts and intent.
- The SSU is impartial and will deliver whatever you have ordered, good or bad.
- The real, eternal you is your Spiritually Existing Love Form, your SELF.
- Your SELF manifests in to the 4D universe as an energy field that drives your body.
- You are an energy field that has a body, not a body that has an energy field.
- Looking at things the other way round is a good habit. Doing a 'one-eighty' can reveal that a problem is usually an opportunity in disguise.
- Your body is your vehicle, get a wellness check and keep it well serviced

INTERESTING TIMES

Demand much of yourself and expect little of others. Thus you will be spared much vexation. Confucius

There is an old curse that runs: "May you live in interesting times." That this was considered a curse might well surprise you. I'd like to explain my understanding of why this is so. The reason it was considered a curse was that interesting times would be an unending source of distraction and attachment. There would be pleasant as well as unpleasant experiences to occupy the senses, but it would all be beyond your control. You would be diverted from the true mission and purpose of any human lifetime. That reason and purpose of life would therefore never get recognised, started or completed. To those wise sages of the dim past "mission *not* accomplished" was truly a fate to be avoided at all costs!

Now that most of us are clearly living in interesting times, it would seem those sages knew what they were talking about. Unfortunately most of the participants in these interesting times are not only prevented from getting on with their mission; they don't even know they have one. Life is just so complex and full of stresses and distractions. The average person is probably finding it all so 'real' and is so involved in struggling to keep bills paid, relationships on track and trying to survive and stay even partially 'well'.

From perspective possible to those who have transcended the illusions of modern 4D life it's obvious that survival and wellness are not the same thing. No, there are many, many survivors out there who have managed to keep ahead of the material game. They have the toys, the wealth and the status but I can see that most of them are quite poor in terms of their wellness. The true state of the bodymind of so much of humanity is far below its potential. It's also clear that for so many people life is bringing forth all the things that they don't want, rather than those things they desire. This means that they have lost the knowledge of how their very existence in this 4D universe shapes it and creates the objects and circumstances they experience. Therefore they have no ability to turn their circumstances around and create differently for themselves and their world.

So my mission calls for me to help everyone recognise just how little control or personal power they have to claim their freedom, wellness and destiny while they are caught up in the web and illusions of interesting times.

Studying and applying knowledge from a book like this because your life isn't what you want it be is a great and valid motive. Embarking on the journey of self-discovery and realisation of your true nature and power because your life sucks and you hate your job, don't have enough money, have been abused or whatever, is a very good reason. You have my full support on the journey to sorting out whatever it is that you feel your life needs or can well do without.

It's not an easy path to travel, as the world of interesting times is a very noisy, distracting and dangerous place indeed. Today everyone is bombarded with stimuli and distractions from so many different media. In a single day, from the moment you wake up until the moment you go to sleep, you are saturated with transmissions from radio, television, mobiles, computers, games consoles, advertising, news and contact with more people than your great grandparents would see in an entire year! If you pay too much attention to all the stuff aimed at you then you will be so totally distracted. There is so much stuff that doesn't actually serve you and your SELF that is keeping you entertained, amused, stressed and busy. It is stuff that will seek to distract, block, oppose and even destroy your inner being's (SELF's) attempts at communicating with you and unlocking your true potential.

Being aware of the existence of these "interesting times" is not enough. It takes the conscious vigilance and consistent effort of 'mindfulness' to avoid the ancient curse. Knowing this is what should motivate you in your efforts to re-connect to your SELF and become free of the illusions of these interesting times. Put like that it sounds simple enough but it isn't easy.

There again you might think that living in these interesting times is perfectly okay. If you place value on your current conditions at home, work and in your relationships with others you might not want any of this shaken or stirred. You might be feeling that there's no benefit to be had from questioning your current state of existence and prefer not to rock the boat.

Well that is up to you, but I would have to say that you have created a comfort zone and are satisfied to live within it. If that's so then you can read this book like you've read so many others and carry on regardless. Remain as you are, or more importantly, as the illusions allow you to think you are.

If you realise that you have created and maintained a comfort zone but now recognise that comfort and progress towards power and freedom are not the same thing, then I congratulate you. You have just made an important and empowering observation that has the potential to start identifying and removing what you don't want in life so you can start attracting and utilising what you do want. That's as good a way to start out with your mission as any other.

So what is this *mission*, this prime purpose of every human's 'being'?

Your mission is to become FREE and re-connect with your true SELF. To get free from the illusions, the programmes and the negative thoughts you currently operate with. To free yourself from the illusion of being separated from all creation. To be able to choose how you act with full awareness of the consequences for yourself and other sentient beings.

Read it again and see there is an absence of the long philosophical meandering you've been programmed to expect. No, that's your lot in just five sentences. Not much really is it? That's because it's the truth and it's simple. As a wise Native American Chief once observed, "*It takes few words to speak the truth*". As you move along this journey you will soon recognise that the things that somehow you KNOW to be true are always simple. No great intellect or specialist knowledge is required because you are born with the necessary connection to truth within you.

So perhaps we ought to spend a few moments pondering a small but extremely pertinent question: *if it's so simple how did billions of bright, talented members of humanity get it so badly wrong?*

Everyone has had a lot of help in complicating it. To be fair much of that complication was created long before you decided to make an entrance into this part of creation. After all, these are very much the "interesting times" of that ancient curse. You've also had many very powerful illusions sold to you so that your own perception of what "to get free" means is probably going to need some work. But that's okay. The process has to begin somewhere and gaining at least some insight into the illusory nature of so much that is perceived as "true" or "real" is a good starting point.

In the film "The Matrix" which you may have heard of, character is called Neo. In the film he had several clues that all was nov as it appeared and felt to be. It is often likely to be the little things that trigger your internal radar. Being told that certain prayers will not be heard because they are the wrong faith. Finding out that true ownership is really about letting go. These are examples of a starting point that, once experienced and recognised, provokes some powerful responses. Starting to see through the illusion stirs up feelings and often uncovers negative emotions that have been carefully swept under the carpet!

The real value of a strong emotional response to some newly sensed truth is in its potential to stimulate some kind of action. So any feelings that you have about what has been, and will be, revealed in this book can be a useful call to action. You need to realise that if you always do what you've always done; you will always get what you always got.

So if you don't like your present circumstances it's pointless doing nothing in the hope that things will change. To change your circumstances, your life, you have to change yourself.

Now hearing that brutal truth can sometimes upset people. If that's so I am not going to apologise for telling the truth. It's perfectly natural to be angry, sad or confused by certain elements of this teaching when they are put before you. Simply use that emotion as juice to fuel action and spur you on.

Why not approach things from the angle of being an adventure? I find each day, no matter how challenging, to be an adventure and a source of excitement and amusement. It's absolutely okay to be on the "mission" but also having fun! Accepting that the primary cause for all that you don't want and don't enjoy in your life is in fact down to you and your own thoughts, actions and inaction is great for getting you on track. It is not about fixing the blame but fixing the problem. To progress you need to accept your responsibility for everything in your life and also your responsibility to change things for the better.

That is the challenge for many today. They have to stop looking elsewhere for the answers and the solution. This aimless searching is not only distracting them from their true potentials it is also dangerous. They look for the answers within others who usually have as many challenges and problems of their own. There is nothing wrong with mutual support and you can get useful answers that way. But the final solution, the application of the answers is for you and you alone.

It is a good thing for you to spend time and share thoughts with people who are in accord with your own wants and interests. I actively encourage students to surround themselves with good people who have similar interests and intentions. You need to be around people who are on the same wavelength as it were. But you need to know that it is no use putting your life and destiny in someone else's hands for no other person on earth holds the key to your best life and destiny. That key is within you and it always has been.

Equally you can help and support others, give answers but you cannot apply them on their behalf. Besides, should you take a splinter out of another's eye whilst you have an enormous plank stuck in your own? Isn't it better to get the plank out of your own eye first? Sadly there are plenty of very poorly sighted "teachers" out there, complete with eyes full of planks, firmly convinced they can see the way well enough to lead the rest. As Obi Wan Kenobi says in one of the Star Wars films, "Who's more the fool, the fool or the fool that follows him?" He has a point.

GOOD VIBRATIONS
To have peace in one's soul is the greatest happiness.

To have the Law of attraction as your ally you need to understand what your true nature and power is. You, like everyone else, are continually creating things and circumstances through your thinking. The SELF Service Universe operates by the Law of Attraction and it is impartial and impersonal. It responds to the energy of your dominant thoughts and feelings.

At the simplest level you can say it is all a matter of vibrations. At any moment the sum total of your thoughts and feelings are a vibration in the energy field of the universe. If we use a musical analogy we can imagine there are billions of 'notes' on the universe's keyboard. Some notes, when sounded together, produce a beautiful and positive effect. Others when combined make a nasty and negative sound. The first is harmony and the latter is discord.

Now let's just think about a great piece of classical music that is being played by a large orchestra. At any point in time there can be a huge number of different notes being played by instruments of all shapes, types and sizes. But the overall effect can be a magnificent and totally uplifting harmony. The conductor can, out of all that sound, instantly pick out any single instrument and any wrong notes! They stand out by breaking the harmony you see?

Every moment of your life you are thinking, imagining, running mental programmes and feeling. So you are constantly creating and transmitting vibrations that reflect this. If your overall vibration is positive and in harmony then you are attracting harmony and positivity into your life. But let's not forget the other side of the coin here, if you are overall producing a negative, discordant vibration guess what you are attracting?

Can you imagine what the dominant thoughts and feelings of six billion humans might be at any point in time? Just think what vibrations are being transmitted through the universe and what a racket it might be! More to the point what might the collective vibration of humanity be ordering up as a bulk delivery!

You see we all have enormous power to affect our personal surroundings and circumstances. We have power that doesn't just impact on us but can, and does, impact on those around us and our world. But we are unskilled in its use and we need to sort this out. That way we can reduce our part in creating the things our lives and world do not want.

By understanding the influence we have on this reality and then gaining control we can consciously act for the good of others as well as for ourselves. We also gain the power to deal with the *causes* of the world's ills. Let's not hide the fact that we have all contributed in some way to environmental damage. We know that thoughts become things even when bad. All the pollution from industry and individuals began somewhere as thought. Someone somewhere thought it was okay to build huge gas-guzzling automobile engines that produce piosonous exhuast fumes. And others thought it was okay to use them to get about instead of walking. We all have a part to play in the negative aspects of life on earth at this time.

If we don't get to grips with this fundamental aspect of our nature we will spend our lives tolerating that which we don't want and spend energy and time sorting out problems and troubles instead of learning how to not attract and cause them. I call it the "Repair and Repent rather than Prepare and Prevent" syndrome. When we are all so chemically and genetically damaged through our effects on our environment that we cannot find our way back, repenting is all we'll be able to do.

You might say, "we probably deserve our fate". But it is not just *we* who are at risk is it? When *Homo Sapiens* finally checks out of Hotel Earth, what will they leave behind? Don't the dolphins, apes, birds, trees, and flowers, in fact every *non-human* life form, also have a fundamental right to exist too?

It would be so much better to use our power individually and collectively to create and sustain positive vibrations. That way we could "Prepare and Prevent so we don't Repair and Repent". In the meantime we carry on producing discord and many other living things are paying the ultimate price for our lack of standard and failure to understand our influence on the 4D universe.

Global warming and climate change is not some myth it's a direct result, the effects of causes humans created. But we are powerful beings and we very well might get the land, or the sea, back to its former glory in so many years. However, we must decide and get on with it.

If the birthright, of every man, woman and child is to be *free* to grow, develop and realise their potential, doesn't that selfsame freedom equally apply to all other living things? Of course it does. The "needs of the many" applies to all life forms and there are still more of them than there are humans. That's why it's vital for you to get the plank out of your own eyes. Then you can make the effort to see beyond the usual "we can fix it" and "it's not my fault" mentality and accept that to many living things it's ultimately lethal. Ask a White Rhino or a gentle Mountain Gorilla if you can get to one in time

You should not waste a moment. You need to understand that the only time and place you have available for taking any kind of action is *Here and Now.* Waiting for a better tomorrow or living in the comfort of the past renders you unable to act. Yesterday is always gone and tomorrow never comes. Only by seizing each passing slice of *Now* and acting appropriately can anyone make a difference. *Now* and there's the possibility of action, *now* and it's gone.

We humans have, as a species, always known our connection to our world and our power to work with or against nature. Modern living and technology has made us forget much of this but there are some amongst us who still remember. Our grasp of human history seems to be pretty uncertain even for the last couple of thousand years or so. However, there are humans on the planet who are direct descendants, still in the same land, of people who walked the surface of the earth over 50,000 years ago. These include the Aboriginal people of Australia.

There are those among them who are the last carriers of "the telling of things" as passed from parent to child for all those thousands of years. Just as many species of animals have already been made extinct and taken with them diversity that we will never see, so are some tribes of the Aboriginal peoples now fading away and their incredible wisdom is fading with them. This is a loss of data and the ways of things here in the 4D that unacceptable.

Let me share some ancient perspective on humanity and its relationship to the world and the cosmos with you. I want to share some words with you as they were spoken by Big Bill Neidjie of the Bunitj people of the Kakadu national park in the Northern Territory, Australia. Fortunately this and other wisdom telling from Big Bill was recorded back in 1983.

These are powerful words spoken by a simple aboriginal man who lived in harmony with nature. Remember that it takes few words to speak truth and read these powerful words:

"Our story is the land.
It is written in those sacred places.
My children will look after those places,
that's the law.
Dreaming place...you can't change it,
no matter who you are.
No matter you rich man,
no matter you King.
You can't change it"

This sense of oneness with the land, the Earth, is something that so many modern humans have lost. It is time to reconnect to this planet, this home of ours. In once again sensing our true connection to this world how could we then continue to tread upon it with such disregard and disrespect? Climate change and pollution are now enormously destructive forces that will, if unchecked, have drastic effects on the planet and all life.

We don't have to see the challenge when it's far too late to do anything about it. It IS possible for humans to live, and live to a decent standard without leaving indelible imprints on the land and life. Big Bill and the Aboriginal peoples of the Australian continent know that their life impacts on the earth but they can co-operate with nature in the process.

Thinking about this relationship with the land Big Bill had this to say:

This earth....
I never damage,
I look after.
Fire is nothing,
Just clean up.
When you burn,
New grass coming up.

That mean good animal soon...
Might be goose, long-neck turtle, goanna, possum.
Burn him off...
New grass coming up,
New life all over.

I don't know white European way.
We, Aborigine, burn...
Make things grow.
Tree grow,
Every night he grow.
Daylight...
He stop.
Just about dark...
He start again.
Just about morning I .look.
I say,
'Oh, nice tree this,'

Please also consider the words of another simple and wise man who predated Big Bill. These words come from a Native American leader called Chief Seattle. He said these words back in 1853 when the white settlers were entering into their "treaties" with the indigenous tribes with the sole aim of seizing and legitimising "ownership" of the land.

"If we sell you land, you must remember that it is sacred, and you must teach your children that it is sacred and that each ghostly reflection in the clear water of the lakes tells of events and memories in the life of my people. Man did not weave the web of life: he is merely a strand in it. Whatever he does to the web, he does to himself."

I also offer these other words of wisdom for your consideration:
The Great Spirit is in all things.
He is in the air we breathe.
The Great Spirit is our Father, but the Earth is our Mother.
She nourishes us. That which WE put in the ground She returns to us.
Big Thunder (Bedagi). Wabanaki Algonquin

They pulled out the leaves
Took out our branches
Cut away our trunk
But could not touch our root
And since it's there
Our strength returns
The Kogi (Elder Brother)

And finally:
When all the trees have been cut down,
When all the animals have been hunted,
When all the waters are polluted,
When all the air is unsafe to breathe,
Only then will you discover you cannot eat money....
Cree Prophecy
Key points to remember:
- Interesting times divert and distract us from our purpose and mission here in the 4D.
- Survival and wellness are not the same thing.
- Many have forgotten how their presence in the 4D shapes their circumstances.
- Your mission is to become FREE and reconnect with your true SELF.
- It takes few words to speak truth.
- Feelings, even negative ones, can be a strong call to action.
- It's better to take the plank out of your own eye before attempting to take the splinter out of the eye of someone else.
- It is not just the right of humans to be FREE but also for all sentient beings and life forms, each to their own potentials.
- We are all connected to this world, to the web of life. In harming our planet we harm all living things and ourselves.
- The only place and time to make difference is here and now.

NOTES, IDEAS AND SCRIBBLES

BORN FREE?

From the Unreal lead me to the Real; From Darkness lead me to Light!

Brihad-aranyaka Upanishad

To get what you want from the SELF Service Universe you have to be able to place your order without any negative thinking. The vibrations of your order must be in harmony with what you really, really wanted to manifest. This means that your thoughts, words and feelings must all be in agreement about what you want. If there is any discord, a wrong note, you'll be sabotaging your order. Once again you'll be positively wishing but negatively thinking. That is why you usually get what you don't want. You are attracting the things, people and circumstances that you really, at the level of your true SELF, do not want. That has to change but to change it requires you to be free.

You probably never realised you weren't *free*. You are in for more than a few surprises when you begin to see what has been done to you and by you, quite often without your knowledge or consent. It's vital that you realise just how many of your thoughts, ideas, hopes, principles and dreams are *not really yours* at all. In fact a great many of the thoughts, emotions, habits and reactions that you consider your own were *programmed* into you. They're illusions of "self" and free will that are an implanted part of your brain's software and will run their course when triggered.

You don't run or own these programmes; they own and run you. These programmes determine so much of what happens in a person's lifetime. When identified with too strongly some programmes become the illusory "self" or *Ego*. They take you with them and, as long as they have the power to run unrecognised and unchecked, they stop you from realising who you really are and from being free to act as you really choose. Most of the programmes that are running in people's heads are implanted by big business, parasitical "authorities", parents, childhood experiences, schooling, religion, politics and, ultimately, the bad folks known as 'The Dark Side'.

What most people do not realise is a simple and powerful truth: what a person thinks affects reality. So having programmes that generate negative thoughts and attitudes is not something to dismiss. Your dominant thoughts radiate out through the universe and eventually bring results to you. Whatever you think about today is already on its way to you. We'll look at this in more detail later but it is important that you understand that this quantum universe is impersonal and doesn't ignore any thoughts that have a certain amount of energy behind them.

To the universal energy that permeates all things at the quantum scale (that is smaller than the smallest particles) everything from subatomic particles to atoms, molecules, cells, bodies right up to planets and galaxies is simply a potential waiting to manifest. We exist in a universe formed from limitless energy and possibilities. All things and all thoughts are forms of energy. We already know that the SELF Service Universe operates in such a way that thoughts make things.

If you can hold something in your mind you can eventually hold it in your hand. As an inventor with Patents to my name I know this as fact. But consider this, if you generate negative thoughts, if you spend energy thinking and focusing on the things that you don't want, guess what? The universe will eventually use the formless quantum field to bring it into being.

With that in mind can you see why the prime objective of your mission to become *free* is achieved by the process of identifying, understanding and dismantling as many of those implanted programmes and negative thought processes as possible?

You need to do this so that the real driver of the bodymind, your SELF, can work through you and allow you to see, assess, think and act appropriately in this 4D universe without error or deviation.

It will amaze you how quickly turning the way you approach your daily life and its challenges from a negative mental viewpoint to a positive one will improve things for you. To change your life and circumstances you have to change your thinking. You need to stop being an unwilling passenger on the journey through your life and get into the driving seat of your bodymind. Well in truth you, the real you, is already there but being held back from the controls sometimes.

That driver of your bodymind vehicle is the real SELF, which stands for Spiritually Existing Love Form. Your SELF is the immortal and eternal spark of spirit that chose to be in the classroom of physical human existence in order to take the curriculum and eventually graduate. Your SELF has its origins in the Great Spirit, Creator, God or any other name that feels appropriate according to your cultural and spiritual attitudes. Your eternal SELF is a fragment of the Great Spirit within the universal quantum energy field and its nature is LOVE. It is the self-aware and eternal spark of the Great Spirit's love force that underpins all of creation in all dimensions (levels of vibration). Your SELF exists in the higher dimensions beyond space and time as experienced in the 4D universe.

Just as a personal computer on an office desk could be seen as an individual unit but also may be the visible part of a huge network, your SELF is far more than that part which appears in the 4D physical plane. Through a computer screen one can, via a suitable modem, access the World Wide Web and bring information and images in front of oneself from anywhere on the globe. The human brain and energy centres are the physical 4D circuitry and 'modem' that can access the infinity of creation at the quantum field level wherein the SELF's true energy pattern and cosmic consciousness resides.

However, just as software is the controlling factor of any computer, the programmes or biological software within your brain and energy circuits control what you the driver currently can and cannot do. You might press the right buttons but are you getting the right answers?

You see your brain is your physical form's hard drive and central processor. It has virtually unlimited memory capacity and its true processing capabilities have never been fully charted. With the billions of connections and quantum processors encapsulated in your brain your actual power to think, process and visualise in the 4D universe is probably limitless. Which makes it a real shame that most humans are utilising so little of the brain's power.

I have heard it said that we use well below even ten percent of our brain's capacity and abilities. If the capacity is virtually limitless how can anyone know what 100 percent is? So forget any idea of percentages. just recognise how little we use of an incredible and unlimited resource!

The programmes that you and others around you have installed in this biological hard drive have a profound and inescapable impact on you as long as they are running unchecked. They also limit your ability to access or be aware of your SELF and its potentials. That is why I have already emphasised the importance of the need to develop the awareness and ability necessary to identify, understand and then remove those programmes and negatively charged thoughts that do not serve you and your SELF.

When you become free from your programmes you also become free to see their sources and intent. The "scales fall from your eyes" revealing a SELF and a world that are both very different to what you had previously perceived them to be. There are various labels for identifying this process such as Self-Realisation and Enlightenment. What you call it doesn't matter that much because if you DO it, then the labels also become seen for what they are. The process also brings into sharp focus the spectrum of good and evil, light and dark as it manifests in your world. It allows you to utilise your compassion and to assess freely, without any external influence or hidden agendas, what is good and appropriate, and what is inappropriate and evil.

Yes, evil *does* exist and it's alive and well and living in your world right now. It is everything that is against life, opposes personal freedom, restricts growth and opposes light and love. Not only does such darkness thrive in this world gone mad; it is, in fact, pretty close to owning it. After all, you can't have failed to see the almost countless examples and demonstrations of the injustice, oppression and unfairness around the world. But there again maybe your programmes just haven't allowed you the time, clarity and opportunity to really *see* what's going on. After all, there are those who have a vested interest in distracting and misleading you so that your Spiritually Existing Love Form won't establish communications with your bodymind and you will remain unaware of a great many things that are holding you back

How can it be that you can feel free when clearly others around you are not? Is it because you can vote, travel, buy what you want, say what you like, get fat or thin if you want to, get married, have a family, buy a house, a car or go on holiday? Does your vote *really* change anything? Can you truly travel where you like? Do you know how many laws, powers and authorities there are in so-called "free society" that, at someone else's convenience can restrict and prevent all of the above, that can enter your home without your consent?

More importantly, whose definition of *wrong* is the one that counts and wields the power? Is it yours or someone else's?

Unfortunately so many people have been so totally distracted by the many programmes running them throughout their lives that these fundamental questions never get asked. Indeed, as far as I can tell, great numbers of your fellow human travellers through these dark years are blissfully unaware that anything is other than it should - or could - be.

Do you accept something as factual and true simply because you saw it on your television, heard it on the radio or read it in a newspaper?

Can you often detect a "blurring" of the facts and truth in the things you are told and shown by people presented as "authorities" or "in the know"?

Just like Neo inside the Matrix seeing the same black cat cross the doorway twice in a few seconds, do you sometimes feel something's not quite right with YOUR particular reality? If so, how *free* do you feel now?

If you are having difficulty with this line of thought it is not something bad or wrong. You are not going to be judged by me. You are this way because you have been programmed to be so. Therefore you've not quite seen certain dark things for what they are. The only difference is that now, with a little help, you might just begin to know it. Knowing how the programmes in your head work is the first step to shaking off the blinkers and chains you didn't even know were there. It's actually simple - but it isn't easy!

Luckily for as many of you as want it, help *is* at hand. That is why you are being given the chance to learn about where you are, how you got here, where you should be going and how to start the journey that will take you there. All you really need is the determination to sign up for a life-changing adventure that will peel away the layers of illusion, misconception, dishonesty, programming and anything else that stops you from becoming a compassionate being with wellness, true "free will" and the power to exercise it.

I am giving you the method to help yourself and your SELF to become free and determine what your life brings. If you apply the simple teaching you could, if you choose, do any of a million things acting as a *free* being accessing the incredible power that is yours and everyone else's by universal law.

Make the decision to begin making changes. If you want your life and your circumstances to change then you have to change your thinking. This cannot be said enough times and I am going to keep on saying it throughout this book. It is my way of helping you overwrite some of your negative programmes with something more useful. It is a fact that if you continue to do what you have always done you will continue to get what you always got. It really is that simple.

You have to accept that things, beginning with you, have to change. They have to change NOW! You must make that decision which isn't a comfortable thing to do. It can also be quite difficult to get started. But having decided to stop sabotaging your positive wishing through negative thinking means you have given yourself no other choice.

Making a decision means that you have cut yourself off from any other course of action that isn't in harmony with what you decided. The word decision comes from a root word that means to 'cut away'. That is how you need to approach your decision-making. Do so knowing that you can 'cut away' from all the programmes, habits and negative factors that have prevented you from living the life you want and deserve as an eternal energy playing in this 4D material realm.

Realise that aside from the procrastinators, who really never make any decisions at all, there are usually only two kinds of decision-makers in this world. There are those who take a long time to make a decision but then take only a short time to change or undo it. Then there are those who make decisions very quickly and then take a very long time, if ever, to change or undo them. Take a moment to think about that will you?

It might surprise you to know that it is the latter group who make the most difference, earn the most money and get the most of what they want out of life. So you should begin to look at your current decision making and invest in learning how to be an effective decision-maker. There are some excellent programmes available to help you with your decision-making and you can check them out at *www.bobproctor.com* or *www. lifesuccesscoach.com*

This book helps you locate the key that turns the lock on the door that leads to a newer brighter future. I haven't placed it here before you because I'm better than you are and certainly not because I'm a selfless and holy soul. I am like you and have faced what you must face and that is my only true qualification as your guide on this adventure. I give this teaching to you because I can. I give it because I *freely* decided to do so. But most of all I want you to read and understand what I have learned because getting you in touch with your SELF can really make a difference.

Key things to consider from this chapter:

- Much of what you consider to be your thoughts and attitudes are in fact programmes installed by others such as parents, teachers, religion, politics etc.
- You don't run the programmes, they run you, often below your consciousness.
- What a person thinks affects reality here in the physical universe.
- Thoughts make things but your programmes often see that those things are not what you actually wanted.
- Your Spiritually Existing Love Form is the true driver of the bodymind vehicle.
- Your SELF is the immortal and eternal spark of spirit that chose to be in the classroom of physical human existence in order to take the curriculum and eventually graduate.
- Our brains offer almost limitless potential and processing power of which we use such a tiny amount.
- Decisions are vital. Making a decision means cutting yourself off from any other course of action.
- Learn to appreciate the power of decisions and become an effective decision-maker.

NOTES, IDEAS AND SCRIBBLES

THERE'S SOMETHING YOU SHOULD KNOW

So long as sentient beings remain, so long as space remains, I will remain in order to serve, or in order to make some small contribution for the benefit of others. Shantideva.

It is time to build your understanding of your true nature and the power you possess to manifest the life you want. This understanding requires some explanation regarding matters of energy and life. These two subjects are quite involved and I propose to only give a simplified introduction to them in this current volume. There's also the matter of language and how we communicate with words. Much of the teaching can be experienced by demonstration without too much verbalisation. In the meantime, through the medium of the written word, I have to do it this way.

The language written or spoken is very important because certain words we use are the keywords for fundamental principles. For example, 'compassion' is more than just a word. It is a principle and quality that has to be integrated – to become a part of the way one lives and acts. In saying the word 'compassion' we must have the discipline and awareness to make the word a total communication containing energy, emotion, thought and understanding. It has to become a vibration that is in harmony with our intent.

When you recall that your thoughts and written goals are delivered through words you begin to see that empowering them with the right vibration is going to improve your results. The SELF Service Universe is quite often in a situation where it hears what you are saying but must act on the energy of the actual vibrations you transmit. That is how you can be specific about what you want but still get something else.

What you have to understand is the something else is what was intended via your programming and beliefs and encoded into the overall vibration accordingly. So putting intent and power behind your words to ensure that there is only a positive note that is in harmony with your wants and feelings is kind of important! I think I need to expand on this a little so you are clear on this point.

Words become very powerful once they become totally identified with precise and consistent patterns within one's mental and emotional states.

You can say something or you can say it with feeling. You can, and often do, say things that you do not mean. Guess what? Other people around you may not know this but the universe does.

Prayer as words that are meant and intended, supported by belief, tend to carry a clear vibration and can be an incredibly powerful thing that has an impact on its surroundings. It is known amongst certain adepts that a precisely controlled and projected word can have very real effects on others and their environment. Masters, Shamans and beings of power understand this truth. We discuss its properties via a formula that goes: every thought has a shape, that shape has a sound, that sound has a word and that word has power.

Many long dead languages were created on this basis of mental vibration and sound vibration being precisely modulated to generate true meaning. Some ancient tongues have survived and in the hands of Masters words from them can alter consciousness, heal, harm and even alter the state of matter.

Today Sanskrit scholars realise that every individual syllable of that venerable language is mathematically and vibrationally formulated so the 'sum' of key words have a direct relationship to their meaning. This is the simple fact behind the power of some Sanskrit Mantras to actually create 'siddhis' (magical yogic powers) if the practitioner masters them.

I trust that is enough for you to get the point. I do not intend to say more on this subject in this current work for various reasons. Not least being a concern that should a dark side politician, for example, become reasonably educated and practised in this subject and its usage, they could gain great power and influence over others. It has happened in the past, as students of Adolf Hitler's rise to power will recognise. It is perhaps less known that Adolf Hitler put a great deal of energy and effort into researching the occult. Along the way he clearly gained a grasp of the power of language to create embedded commands and alter moods. Could it happen again? I simply note the fact that the modern media have already created many 'new' words and successfully programmed a large number of people with their meaning.

Now we must move on to explore another use of language. This is, in certain ways, equally full of power. It is as old as human language itself and is simply the art of telling stories. More precisely it is the art ıssing wisdom from person to person and generation to generation simply by verbalising myths, parables and legends.

In many cultures, even after the invention and dissemination of written language, the most vital tribal wisdom and history was not written down in any form. It was passed down the timeline by word of mouth in the ancient art of story telling. Carefully trained individuals would pass on their 'telling' to the next generation in its original pure form with each generation adding the next chapters of the history and knowledge. This meant that you needed to able to listen, remember and recall without overlaying any of your own opinions, thoughts or impressions. Changing so much as a syllable was out of the question!

Today we have many different methods/technologies for recording, storing and retrieving our knowledge and histories. We also have the means to also make subtle and sometimes not too subtle changes to the records and, over time, those changes become the new accepted and authoritative source.

The modern media is a powerful device for serving either truth or falsehood and can create extremely convincing scenarios. The media can put bias on events to reinforce certain programmes inside people's heads and therefore influence their behaviour. The advancing technology makes it harder and harder to see the joins and cut through the hype and gloss.

One form of modern communication is the World Wide Web and more specifically the Internet.

The origin of the Internet is an interesting story in light of our current subject. The Internet is a direct outcome of what has become a globe-spanning network of computer networks. That is an inter-linking of computers all over the Earth (and actually now above in satellites) using telephone lines, fibre optic links and radio frequencies. In the Cold War of the last century the reliance on computers to run the defence network of missile launch sites and bomber commands all over the USA and Europe was susceptible to any attack that crippled any of its computers. The idea of linking computers in local networks (several computers around a room or building that shared information and resources via cable links) was already known and in use. The new idea was using the USA's vast telephone and military communications infrastructure to allow computers to dial-up each other via different telephone lines if any one was disabled. The use of computers as telephone exchanges that could detect the loss of a line and switch to another was born.

The military's Advanced Research Projects Agency (ARPA later to become DARPA with the 'D' standing for Defence) oversaw the system then called the ARPAnet. Then the idea of speeding up military research projects by eliminating wasted lines of research and avoiding costly duplication of effort had the ARPAnet linking into the laboratories and University libraries too.

Soon it was possible for the larger businesses and organisations to also have their computers networks linked to each other and into the ARPAnet. Sharing fiscal and scientific data and having computers swapping files 'on-line' was becoming quite routine and so the number of networks grew. The birth of the world wide web of the Internet was this gradual merging of different networks until a 'network of networks' spanned the globe.

Of course the old technique of actually putting a telephone handset into a special cradle so the computer could dial into the network became obsolete. The external and then internal Modems got smaller, cheaper and faster. The software to make the interface between the World Wide Web and the user got friendlier. The now familiar 'windows' you use on your computer screen to understand and control your PC were a major factor in bringing the computer, and the Internet, to more and more non-military, non-big business, users. Of course there was money to be made and the businesses and organisations that made their computer servers available to anyone who could dial-in saw how fast the whole thing was growing. And so it got bigger, faster and, ultimately, completely out of anyone's control.

The Internet is currently without political, religious, racial or moral limitations, which makes it a dangerous loose cannon in all directions. The military and big business have discovered that the two-way nature is a real threat because the public has got a lot smarter now. So the Internet is a massive resource for anyone with a computer and access to the World Wide Web. Anyone with an agenda has a platform to shout it from. Any perversion can be catered for in some way. Whatever you want to know you can probably find out there in cyberspace. But please be careful and exercise discretion as to what you accept as factual or true. There's a lot of self-serving material out there looking for others to accept it as truth and even to act upon it.

In Moses' day the media chosen for the job were apparently a burning bush and several tablets of stone. But it worked didn't it? Now it's a lot easier to carry and disseminate information. It's also just as convincing as any burning bush or stone tablet to those who are programmed to believe and accept it.

The truths we are seeking are protected by living Masters and transmitted from generation to generation in ways that prevent such tampering. But we also use whatever media will bring the teaching to a wider audience, keeping a wary eye on it of course! So this book is just one line of communication that will work for some. For others there will be other ways of delivering what they need to know. Whatever the medium being used, this teaching is being brought to people's attention simply because it is time.

There's not much time in which to undo so much damage to the Earth and its inhabitants. That's at least one thing that many scientists, politicians and cultures are finally becoming aware of. In fact there would appear to be a growing acceptance of the proposition that there is much to be done to re-establish lost values, forgotten truths and undo the damage sustained by the planet and many of its inhabitants.

This isn't something that we can leave to someone else either. We each live here too and as living systems we are all at risk from the damaging chemical, electromagnetic and environmental factors that are all around us. It's not much use relying on wishful thinking either. Most people continually undo their positive wishing through negative thinking. Indeed, as you know, the overall negativity has an effect that brings to us the very things our positive wishing doesn't want. So we need to get to grips with our individual and collective power and ability to impact on the very fabric of our existence here in the 4D universe.

You see you cannot ever be outside the effects of the Law of Attraction. It is always working always delivering what our most dominant thoughts attract. If we keep seeing negative things around us that is our doing. If we meet negative, bad people we know they have become that way is response to their thinking.

The opposite also applies (thanks to the one-eighty again). The key is to decide what kind of people and circumstances we really want. Surround yourself with good people. Form alliances and relationships with people who understand and use their power in the SELF Service Universe for positive results. So you can collectively, through gaining an understanding of this law and applying it consciously, set about attracting better things and circumstances for your world and yourselves.

We all live on this planet so I think we can take time out here from our own personal needs and look at what is going on for planet earth. Don't worry, I will put you back on course for your own needs soon enough.

In 1992 the 'Earth Summit' in Rio de Janeiro was supposed to explore the world's environmental issues and attempt to gain consensus on how to start correcting serious problems. Sadly it failed to persuade enough of the world's national governments to take positive action.

In the same year a powerful was document published entitled the 'World's scientists warning to humanity'. This was no minor publication because over sixteen hundred scientists from 71 countries endorsed the work

However suffice it say that the document's introduction began: *Human beings and the natural world are on a collision course. Human activities inflict harsh and often irreversible damage on the environment and on critical resources. If not checked many of our current practices put at serious risk the future that we wish for human society and the plant and animal kingdoms, and may so alter the living world that it will be unable to sustain life in the manner that we know.*

The scientists went on to cover the various pollutants and environmental factors. They also arrived at a conclusion that *'no more than one or a few decades remain before the chance to avert the threats we now confront will be lost and the prospects for humanity immeasurably diminished'.* As I was editing this paragraph I realised that one of those decades had already passed.

I also heard, at the time of writing this very page, in September 2004, of a leading European scientist's call for the creation of a kind of 'Noah's Ark' on the surface of our moon to hold samples of the DNA of all Earth's life. I had to check it wasn't April Fool's Day before paying any attention to the report. This eminent scientist's reasoning appeared to be that we need to preserve this 'record' of life on Earth because of the increasing and very real likelihood of a chemical, biological or nuclear catastrophe wiping out all life on this planet in the near future. Apparently the European Space Agency has robotic lunar probes quite capable of constructing a domed facility on the moon.

Now I don't just accept what I see or hear. I, as you will hopefully learn to do, run anything like this through several 'filters' before giving it any real attention. I approach these particular technology-based reports from the viewpoint that all new and advanced technology is primarily controlled by the military and secret government agencies around the world. If the 'public' have seen or heard about any kind of advanced technology it has long since outlived its military usefulness and has been superseded by something more advanced.

So getting back to the moon based 'Noah's Ark' matter, the public announcement that we have the technology to have robots build a domed facility on the moon means something else to me. Also I would very much enjoy discovering just how the eminent scientist has arrived at this amazing idea. If we do succeed in wiping out everything on Earth then who, or what, does he think will know and even care enough to retrieve this DNA record? Anyway enough of that! Now we need to look at the matter of energy, which, as I mentioned earlier, is a little bit more involved than other subjects of interest are.

Some reminders from this chapter:

- Every thought has a shape, that shape has a sound, that sound has a word and that word has power.
- Wisdom has been preserved and transmitted for thousands of years through stories.
- The media can put bias on events to reinforce certain programmes inside people's heads and therefore influence their behaviour.
- Most people continually undo their positive wishing through negative thinking.
- Surround yourself with good people.
- We all have a role in helping make our world a better, nicer and safer place for all life and sentient beings.

NOTES, IDEAS AND SCRIBBLES

A CLOSER LOOK AT ENERGY
A great man is one who has not lost his child's heart. Mencius

There is much more to biological life than literally meets the eye. There is more to you than you can currently see. It is becoming common knowledge that all life radiates an energy field around the physical form it inhabits. It is after all, from the 4D scientific viewpoint, a simple fact of physics and biology. The 4D explanation goes like this: life forms of any size or species (even plant life) generate electrical and chemical energy within physical structures in accordance with well-documented physical 'laws'. The electrical energy is conducted through biological structures that have evolved for that purpose, as encoded in the life form's genetic coding of its DNA. These structures are what we call the nervous system. Groups of nerves when stimulating other structures such as muscle fibres can produce phenomena ranging from respiration, locomotion and digestion through to thought, speech and consciousness.

It is a fact that an electrical current cannot flow without creating a field around it. This field is electro-magnetic in nature and its wavelength, frequency and range is subject to well-understood physical laws and can be calculated. It is important that such 'science' of our 4D existence is clear in your mind when we move ahead to look at the trouble our world is facing. If you accept that the above is known to everyone who has influence on the world through science, technology and political regimes you can see how blindingly obvious the truth should be.

All life exists within individual and collective electromagnetic fields of varying strengths, frequencies and range. Ancient yogic science and 'occult' organisations and mystery schools have known of these fields for a very long time indeed. The ability to detect and record them through highly developed human senses – often described as extra-sensory perception – has created some fascinating theories and descriptions.

The yogic scientists recorded these electromagnetic bio-energy fields as 'auras'. They also observed and recorded other distinct energy fields within the aura around the exterior of the human body linked to key physical glands and nerve ganglia. The ancient seers observed these as distinct localised energy fields on the body that were in constant motion. The term they used to label them was 'Chakras' which translates into 'wheels'. We have a modern scientific justification for the existence of an electromagnetic or bio-energetic field surrounding any life form, and the ancient observation of the phenomenon of the Aura and Chakras.

Moving from biological life to technology we come across something similar. You cannot pass an electric current through a circuit without producing a corresponding electromagnetic field. Indeed some technology is only concerned with the work the electricity does but other technology is directly dependant on producing specifically shaped electromagnetic fields. The whole area of radio transmission is concerned with the generation and transmission of electromagnetic fields from one location to another. Think of television, radio and mobile telephones for example.

If any electrical activity is impossible without a corresponding electromagnetic field being generated then we need to look at our modern world. It is a fair assumption that most of you reading this have sat in front of a television, used a microwave oven, called someone on a mobile telephone, been in a car or a train, sat close to a computer screen, used a personal stereo or other audio device. Every single one of these items I mentioned generates and sustains an electromagnetic field that extends – in some case for tens of centimetres – around it. The field from power lines is measurable tens of metres away from the wiring and pylons.

These are all artificial fields of frequencies, wavelengths and energies being generated by technology, not biological life. Such energy fields are not native to the planet. They are not native and harmonising with the magnetic fields of the planet and our sun or indeed with the fields of the planet's native life forms. That means they are not natural to YOU either.

In other words, there is a dense man-made "electromagnetic fog" that envelops the globe today. This electromagnetic fog is so strong and full of unnatural frequencies that it blots out the natural fields of our planet. It is overpowering the naturally generated magnetic fields that are the cocoon that all the variety of Earth's life forms evolved within. In fact this 'fog' radiates out into space for a huge distance. Our television and radio broadcasts, which are part of this fog, are now well beyond the confines of our Solar System.

So why should we be aware of the electromagnetic fog? This fog is creating mutations in the fine circuitry of the energy bodies and genetic codes of virtually all our planet's sentient life forms.

All life on Earth and its genetic codes were evolved and tuned over vast time frames to respond to the naturally occurring magnetic and cosmic energy fields that surrounded and pervaded this globe. The life forms were evolved in accordance with the guiding intelligence of the universal consciousness of the multi-dimensional quantum field. The life forms had to be viable vehicles and sustainable so the environment they manifested in was a crucial part of the equation of life and evolution. All the base operating electrical energies, chemical processes and electromagnetic field outputs of life from cellular level upwards in scale had to function in co-operation with those fields present in the environment surrounding them. The harmonisation of internal and external forces was the secret to establishing and maintaining the incredible bio-diversity of planet earth. Our ability to overpower these natural energy fields with our own artificial electromagnetic fog is only very recent in geological time.

For millions of years the only bio-energy fields and planetary magnetic fields were those naturally occurring. During those millions of years the land, oceans, various minerals and crystal deposits modulated these energies in their vicinity. The development of biological life had its forms and functions evolving through mutations in DNA as a direct response to environment and associated chemical and energetic factors present. The double helix pattern of bonded nucleic acids that manifest as the physical aspect of DNA is indicative of a finer energy structure. DNA is not only a physical molecular structure it is also a microscopic antenna operating on natural electromagnetic wavelengths. Therefore these DNA structures in all biological life are, by nature, very sensitive to close proximity electromagnetic energy fields. In fact at the fundamental level of this physical 4D universe those DNA structures ARE energy fields.

It is a fact that the human body is magnetically and electromagnetically transparent across a broad spectrum. If it weren't then the latest medical scanning technologies simply wouldn't work. Let us just come to a simple conclusion regarding our exposure to the electromagnetic fog: *the basic DNA structures of biological life are not designed to operate in the artificial electromagnetic fields and microwave radiation now penetrating and surrounding the Earth today.* The dancing fields of energy that have been tuned to create and maintain the diversity of biological physical structures are being subjected to the unnatural energies and these can, and do, knock our fields 'out of tune'. This creates (causes) effects to manifest in the physical structures that arise from the natural energy fields that comprise life on earth.

The movement and distribution of metals and chemical elements from their original planetary locations is also a factor for consideration when looking at this subject of natural energy. We are living in a modern world that has mined and removed such huge volumes of minerals and resources from their original and naturally occurring locations. Such activity creates localised warps, hotspots and other unpredictable, unfriendly modifications to the energy fields that once supported and reinforced the genetic patterns of life in the vicinity. I mean unpredictable and unfriendly modifications that impact energetically on DNA across a broad band of wavelengths and frequencies.

In the distant past native people, although perhaps not utilising such modern medical and scientific terms, easily and readily understood this issue. Our ancient ancestors built pyramids, temples and other "sacred architecture" as a means of enhancing these important energy fields on a strictly localised basis. They also used certain metals and crystals in a similar fashion. Recent excavations of very ancient mine workings revealed that the miners carefully re-filled the mines with local material as they backed their way out. This deliberate in-fill after the mines were exhausted or fully worked must have been for a reason. Perhaps they knew that to remove metal ores or minerals created an imbalance in nature and attempted to restore the balance by replacing what they took with other local material.

So with all the mining activity and modifications of environments that modern 'civilisation' has undertaken, what is the impact on the invisible but very influential energy patterns of our world? Millions of people move through the Earth's magnetic field in those metal boxes that we call cars. Many are living near high voltage power lines or breath chemical pollutants. They are also eating unnatural diets. Humans are separating themselves from direct contact with the ground, sitting in front of televisions and computer screens, using millions of mobile phones and microwave devices.

Is it any wonder that so few are truly fit, healthy, natural and have an unadulterated DNA pattern? As a result there are many ailments afflicting and killing today that human science has not yet detected, never mind labelled, classified and investigated. Even those of us who have no disease or disability are not enjoying true wellness.

We are operating on an assumption that the technology we create "serves" us. That it makes our lives better or easier. The truth is far different and once you accept the nature and effects of electromagnetic fog you have to decide what to do. That is the task that faces each and every one of us. We are mistaken in our claim that we inherited this world from our forefathers. No, we are actually custodians of the world and its resources for our descendants. By the way, if you believe in reincarnation then the ramifications are clear: if you mess this world up now, then you are going to have to live with the consequences somewhere in the future when you "come back". Ouch!

How does all this information relate to you the dear reader? It is simple when you realise that you and your physical form are not really matter but energy. Let me explain this as simply as possible. Take a look at your hand. It is solid isn't it? Look at a table. It is solid too. It is harder than your hand but your hand hitting the table testifies to you that both these objects have solidity. At our scale of existence and perception this is so. But the truth is that your hand and the table are energy fields that are operating on a similar scale and vibratory rate and as such can appear solid to each other.

Okay let's move to a finer scale shall we? Get a powerful microscope and examine the back of our solid hand. Now we see beyond skin, beyond even skin cells, now we are looking at molecules that are linking together to form those cells. But look again; those molecules are made up of even smaller bits that are linked somehow. Those bits are atoms and as far as we can tell, they are spheres of electrons whirling around a central nucleus. But wait a moment! These atoms comprise a small core, or nucleus, and an outer set of orbiting electron shells. The rest of the atom is empty space!

At an even smaller scale, the quantum level, the electrons and subatomic particles of the atom's nucleus are not actually even there either. They are probable particles, they are quantum field originated energy frequencies that pop in and out of apparent nothingness with no regard for space and time or for how science would like them to behave. The particles only become detectable and 'real' when the wave function collapses and somehow 'selects' one of a large number of probable locations and states.

The upshot this is that the basic building blocks of classical physics and our universe are mainly the nothingness of empty space and energy that has the probability of being a particle. Albert Einstein worked on his understanding of this matter/energy issue and realised the famous equation $E=MC^2$ which states how mass and energy are interchangeable and demonstrates the energy liberated from even the smallest mass is huge. The energy that is currently creating the physical particles that make up your body is absolutely enormous.

You are a physical body that has mass, size and apparent solidity at our scale of perception. But now I hope you understand that you are actually a fantastic and complex dance of energy. You and everything in the universe are connected. You are not an independent, separate something that is unaffected by what is done to the planet and its sentient beings.

NOTES, IDEAS AND SCRIBBLES

HOW ARE YOU WELLWISE?

As long as you cannot forgive the next man for being different, you are still far from the path of wisdom.

Having considered the matters of energy and electromagnetic fields and have to now deal with their effects. We know that the world is contaminated electromagnetically and chemically, not to mention the climate change effects. It is also true that all things are connected so how do we live with that? I mean that literally, on the assumption that you want to live as long and as well as possible!

I can encourage you with the knowledge that you can do things to lessen the effects of the electromagnetic fog now surrounding and penetrating your physical form. I can show you a few ways but it is up to you put them into practise. We will be looking at your breathing, nutrition and other things later. Please remember that the electromagnetic fog is present every millisecond and will be for the foreseeable future. The chemical pollutants are not going away any time soon either. So the challenge is to change our collective awareness of our relationship with this planet.

You also have to take yourself to a level of wellness that gives you the best possible level of resistance to the harmful environmental factors that are damaging all of us at the chemical, genetic and energetic levels. This matter of wellness is something you need to give your serious attention to. The simple fact is that most humans alive today are operating at a base level in mind, body and spirit that is well below what was average for our ancestors only two hundred years ago. So, what is wellness?

"Wellness is a state of good mental, physical and spiritual health, supported and maintained by proper diet, exercise and beneficial habits. Wellness is when our Bodymind & Spirit are all free from suffering allowing us to have the time, energy and freedom to live the life we want."

In the state of true wellness the bodymind is free from stress, worry or neuroses and is functioning in such a manner as to generate genuine peace of mind and a joyful presence here in the moment. Wellness means we are able to use our mental capacities to their fullest potential allowing us to function freely and successfully in our world and our relationships.

The well bodymind is effectively nourished, well exercised, and has no disease. It sleeps well, eats well and, when damaged, repairs itself quickly and effectively. As such it is full of vitality and is a physical vehicle that allows us to express ourselves as we choose. The well spirit becomes a source of love, wisdom, courage, and strength and, as such, connects us with all living things.

It is therefore important that you take responsibility for obtaining an accurate assessment of your current wellness. Get a clear idea of where you need to make improvements in your nutrition, exercise, hygiene, mental processes and spirituality. At the back of this book I have listed various resources and these include access to wellness information, evaluation and support. Let's be clear about this; your ability to enjoy the life you want is reliant upon you getting your act together and improving your vitality, energy and mental power through optimising your personal wellness. Having the best physical vehicle possible gives you a sound foundation to build a life as a free SELF-aware being that gets what it wants.

Of course the true SELF that manifests through your physical vehicle is, to a great extent, immune to any actual harm from your personal wellness or lack of it. Likewise the SELF cannot sustain any injury from the conditions manifesting in the physical environment of the 4D universe you currently inhabit. Your SELF has a different handicap to deal with. There is currently not a clear line of communication from your SELF through to 4D otherwise you would probably not be reading this or any other book like it. Your SELF knows enough of the 'reality' you experience to eventually force through the message, or intent, to send you looking for the information and methodology to open up the channel properly. Yes, that's the mission again – getting FREE.

Now it should be common sense that the physical vehicle and bio-energetic interface that link it to its SELF and to the 4D environment are not what they used to be. I hope that the previous explanations of the factors forcing mutations in the DNA and energy fields were enough for you to have arrived at this conclusion. But for the sake of clarity I will just confirm that millennia of evolutionary alterations in the human DNA have been compromised by just a few centuries of human 'ingenuity' and technical 'progress'.

It used to take Mother Nature or 'natural selection' thousands of years to make very small changes in the genetic structure of DNA. The modern environment is causing several bits of DNA data to be overwritten in just a few years. This means that the re-write rate for DNA has accelerated in just a few hundred years by a huge factor. A lot of this new code is pure garbage and the DNA has built-in redundancy to prevent much of the replication errors (mutations) from manifesting in the overall physical structure. However some new code gets through and creates mutations.

Your SELF needs your physical bodymind vehicle. It is the only proven means of locomotion and experience you have within the 4D universe. The good news is that your SELF can, if it has enough access, operate through the dimensional interface and inhibit the genetic damage. Moreover, it can in some instances make corrections to the DNA sequencing and actually overwrites some of the bad code.

You can help it in this task by becoming aware of and managing your energy pattern. You can take steps to enhance your genetic 'immunity' to environmental overwriting. But most importantly you can enlist your SELF in this mission by freeing up the system from the illusions and imposed programming that inhibits true communication with your SELF.

With this firmly in mind we need to move ahead through the next few chapters of this work. We are going to explore some very effective methods and strategies. Once you start out on this I need you to know something: bad stuff happens and things sometimes get worse before they get better. It's part of the clearing out process.

I am not trying to worry you or put you off, but I won't lie to you or make any false promises. If you start to break free from your programming, restricting beliefs, the ego and your negative thinking habits and strive to connect to your SELF you will begin to see many things are not as they seemed to be.

Many of the illusions that have kept you 'comfortable' will begin to take on new appearances and natures that will not please you. Be prepared for relationships with others that once seemed eternal and true to also lose their gloss. This can be unpleasant, distressing and uncomfortable to start with. But we get free through application of the qualities of honesty, integrity and commitment. That means not flinching from what you now know to be true, recognising as you will that the truth depends upon where you stand in the NOW and therefore much you once held as true becomes otherwise as you progress. It also means that once you commit to doing something you stick with it for as long as it takes, no matter how hard it becomes or how tiresome.

Commitment isn't staying with something 'as long as it's comfortable and convenient' which is what you will discover it means to many others around you. No, commitment is the principle of staying with something for as long as it takes without any regard as to whether doing so is comfortable or not.

We all know of situations where we have heard people assure us that they are totally committed to whatever was in progress only to see them drop it as soon as the going got tough! Guess what? There have been so many such people who have quit without ever realising that they were within reach of the goal. That's like swimming for ten miles in the fog and giving up without knowing that the finish line was only fifty feet away. The real winners in life already know that there is more to be gained from finding the strength to keep going than from giving up.

I once did some research with a training manager for a company with a large direct sales force. He and I were looking at how the sales force went about getting (or not getting as the case seemed to be) any new business. As the research progressed we were simply astounded by what we discovered. The company's sales people were, on average, making three calls on new prospects they wanted to do business with. The success rate was pretty poor and so the prospecting was costing money with little or no reward. My friend and I found out that a large number of these prospects gave their business to new suppliers after the fifth call. To add insult to injury, the company's competitors were being opportunistic by calling a couple of times after our sales people had quit and were getting the business!

Our people were within two calls of the business but were quitting having made three calls already. Their commitment to prospecting was not what it should have been. In my eyes it wasn't commitment at all because they didn't stay the distance once they were outside their comfort zone. As you can imagine my friend and I explained how this behaviour couldn't possibly make good business sense and changes were made. The interesting thing to consider is that all of these sales people were good professionals who stood to earn some decent commission from gaining new customers. So why would they go to the time, effort and expense of preparing the ground so they could abandon the potential business, and commission, so close to success?

Well of course, to be fair, they didn't know and didn't realise what my friend Keith and I saw to be obvious. Once we knew it was our job to share this knowledge in a clear and understandable manner, backing it up with any re-training and support systems that would increase success. Amazingly enough that is exactly what this book is about in relation to YOUR life success.

I know what's in store for some of you who really commit to the mission and so I have to share it with you. I can only be truthful and tell you this: you are going to have some moments when you really feel like kicking yourself. There will also be times when you would probably like to kick someone else, including me if you could find me in time. Because nobody likes a smart arse do they? The danger of stating the obvious to people who simply didn't see it is that you get a negative reaction.

That is kind of strange and certainly counter-productive if you think about it. Personally I am always extremely grateful when someone has the time, kindness and interest in my welfare to point out something obvious that I have missed. What a gift! Think of the added commissions those salespeople earned once they had been shown the obvious. You can always benefit from getting better and smarter at the job of living in this 4D universe.

Make a commitment to your SELF that you will become free and realise your true nature and potential. You can have the life you want and you can have a very powerful impact in turning away all the things that you do not want. It is entirely up to you and you alone. Do what you have always done and get what you always got or choose to change yourself NOW and thus change your circumstances. If you want to get something different then you have to do and be something different!

I have a response to people who are reluctant to try something new or different. I tell them that they might be the world's greatest Yak Herder but they'll never know until they climb a mountain and start herding Yaks!

Some points from this chapter for your consideration:

- You can do things to lessen the detrimental effects of the electromagnetic fog now surrounding and penetrating your physical form.
- Wellness is a state of good mental, physical and spiritual health, supported and maintained by proper diet, exercise and beneficial habits. Wellness is when our Mind, Body & Spirit are all free from suffering allowing us to have the time, energy and freedom to live the life we want.
- Get a clear idea of where you need to make improvements in your nutrition, exercise, hygiene, mental processes and spirituality.
- There is currently not a clear line of communication from your SELF through to your 4D bodymind.
- Your SELF needs your physical bodymind vehicle, so look after it.
- Many of the illusions that have kept you 'comfortable' will begin to take on new appearances and natures that will not please you once you break away from the programmes.

THIS MIGHT HELP

Life affords no higher pleasure than that of surmounting difficulties, passing from one stage of success to another, forming new wishes and seeing them gratified. He that labours in any great and laudable undertaking has his fatigues first supported by hope and afterwards supported by joy. Samuel Johnson

We have already seen how every living thing has an energy field. Your energy field comprises the fields generated by electrical activity within the brain and physical body, which are measurable with such technology as EEGs and ECGs. It also contains the energy from the zero point quantum field creating all the particles in your body. Analysis of the electrical activity in the human brain shows several quite distinct frequencies and rhythms that are associated with life and consciousness.

I recently read that the energy field output of the human heart is several hundred times more powerful than that of the human brain. That is interesting particularly if we consider the concept of the human heart as being more than just a vital physical organ. The heart has also an association with the finer emotions and qualities of human existence. I often find that I am dealing with people who dwell almost entirely in their heads with only very occasional trips to their hearts. The head is a very useful tool and should be used as such. But one should also recognise the power and relevance of the heart. It is rather like dealing with Mr Spock for the logical, scientifically detached and emotionless duties and with Captain James T Kirk for the feeling, emotional and commanding human stuff! Ideally one would want to be using both aspects in balance.

The aura, or electromagnetic field, that is an integral part of any living organism here in the 4D universe is constantly under attack by unnatural energy fields in the environment. There can be no doubt that every piece of technology that utilises electrical power generates and radiates an electromagnetic field. That is a simple scientific fact and a demonstration of cause and effect in action.

We also know that, unlike the energy patterns and frequencies generated and sustained in nature, these energies radiating from technology are a recently new phenomenon. The man-made electromagnetic fog, when compared to the millions of years of nature and evolutionary progress, is a very last minute arrival. The effects of these artificial energy fields, whether from your computer, television, mobile phone, power lines, power stations, strip lighting, vehicles or any technological source, are as yet not fully understood.

The clustering of various diseases around power stations, pylons and the general level, or rather lack of, wellness in people and nature would seem to indicate that such effects are not beneficial. I say this knowing full well that there's none so blind as those who won't see, or as deaf as those who will not hear.

Well it is fairly obvious that we have developed a world and cultural systems that cannot abandon technology overnight or in any particularly imminent future. Neither can we, in light of the increasing evidence of global climate change, just sit on our hands and carry on regardless. We can see that damage is being done. If we carry on doing what we have always done then we know we will carry on getting what we have always got. That's not good news for many life forms including our own. So we need to consider our options, intelligently assess the appropriate course of action and then implement change.

For all its evils we have to also accept that some technology can and does have its uses. The very sources of energy fields that are damaging our world and us are technologies that can also be tuned and developed to assist us in a positive way. It will take time for us to fully understand and learn to measure and monitor the finer and subtler frequencies and their interaction with us at the genetic and energetic levels. However, if we decide that this is the thing to do then we can begin to make useful changes.

Here in the 4D part of the SELF Service Universe those changes, as an effect, have to have a cause. Like anything else involved with humanity changes have to start, as always, with a single human thought. That thought as cause will have an effect that can manifest as stimulating similar thoughts in others. Eventually the thought will achieve enough power to become manifest as a reality. That is because, as we know, thoughts become things – including actions.

The aim for you, as a concerned inhabitant of planet earth and as someone on a journey to your true nature and SELF, is to avoid dwelling on the negatives of the electromagnetic fog and its effects. Instead you need to have a positive outlook and consider how to fix the problems rather than fixing the blame.

This is important! The SELF Service Universe operates by impersonal laws and responds to thought whether the thought is good or bad. You need to be able to live here in this 4D aspect of creation and on this planet in particular. If you get caught up in focussing on how bad climate change and global warming are you are adding your thought power to the manifestation of bad outcomes. You want to be around a long time and enjoy your life without spending lots of energy just staying alive. So recognise any programming that wants to run along the lines of "Things are bad and are going to get worse" or "this is a global problem I can't make a difference". Spot these and disable them because they are not helpful. If your dominant mental energy is directed at what is wrong, bad or not wanted, that is what is going to manifest. That's positive wishing being sabotaged by negative thinking and programming again. These programmes have the power to make you and your circumstances worse than they have to be. You now know that this is the darker side of your link to the SELF Service Universe, but that can change. Instead focus on positive thoughts such as "We have a lovely world and we can look after it" or " I know I make a difference" or "I am increasing my wellness and no harm can come to me".

In the meantime how can you at least give your body and your energy pattern a boost and offset the effects of the electromagnetic fog? Well there are several things you can do and I am happy to recommend them for your consideration. I discovered some useful and, in my experience, beneficial solutions that you could look at:

Good nutrition is always intelligent. Especially so when our physical systems are under constant attack from stress and negative environmental factors. Now good nutrition isn't just about cramming a few multi-vitamin pills down your throat every day. No, you need to get good protein intake, a balanced diet for fatty acids, fats, carbohydrates, essential enzymes and amino acids. Your physical form has a continuous repair and regeneration function that has to have all the raw materials, the building blocks, on hand at any time to do its job.

You wouldn't expect your car to run without putting fuel in the tank or the engine to stay running smoothly without providing oil and water. So take the same care of your vehicle. You should also make use of natural herbs and naturally derived supplements as necessary for your personal optimum wellness. Antioxidants are becoming more vital as all the free radicals present in our environment increasingly attack and damage the cells of our bodies. Take a visit to www.teameuro.eu/sheridan for a good nutritional solution.

You should drink plenty of water. In fact you should drink more than one and a half litres of water every day. I didn't say drink tea, coffee or soda. You can drink that stuff if you choose but, at the nutritional level that is important to you and your wellness, it does NOT count as water. The average human body uses and loses over 1.5 litres of water a day just by being alive. Aim to drink clean, fresh water throughout the day and make sure your intake is more than 1.5 litres. Take a visit to www.well-wise.co.uk and learn more about wellness evaluation and nutritional support.

Correct breathing is absolutely vital and to assist you I have devoted two chapters to the subject a little further on in this book. Please be sure to study your breathing and, if necessary, carry out the instructions I provide for mastering the complete breath. The benefits to your physical form and to your energy pattern will be obvious after a short while breathing as nature intended you to.

Magnetism is an important natural 4D factor also worthy of consideration. Our blood is a vital tool in oxygenating our tissues, it carries nutrients around our body and removes toxins that accumulate through our daily lives. Poor circulation and uneven magnetic interference can have negative impacts on our wellness. The key element that is carrying oxygen throughout the circulatory system is the haemoglobin in our blood. This is iron-based and has magnetic properties that are the result of millions of years of evolution in the earth's own magnetic field. That field is now overpowered by our technologies and way of life so our blood is not operating at the magnetic signature found in nature.

You can improve circulation and oxygenation by wearing a magnetic bracelet or necklace. A lot of time and research has been carried out to determine the best and most beneficial magnetic field structures. I often wear a magnetic bracelet developed by Bio-Flow. If you want to learn more do an internet search or visit www.ecomagnets.com

Become a proficient and regular <u>meditator</u>. Again this subject gets its fair share of my attention in this book. The key to becoming aware of the mind and the foreign installations, the implanted programmes, is to be found here. The bodymind is, in most people, a very noisy place indeed! We are on a mission to re-connect you to your truest SELF and thereby gain your true power in the SELF Service Universe.

<u>Quartz crystals</u> and other natural treasures from the earth can be utilised in protecting and enhancing your bodymind and energy field. Although it may appear to be an entirely 'new age' thing, crystal healing and the use of natural substances from the earth's mineral realm is very ancient indeed. The piezo-electric effect of quartz crystal is fascinating in itself. Without it most cigarette lighters and gas cookers wouldn't ignite!

Basically the atomic structure of quartz is a well ordered and regular lattice that produces a phenomenon where movement/vibration applied to it as cause, generates an electron flow, electrical discharge, as effect. In others words, hit a quartz crystal and you get electricity out. But this is an equation and so it works either way. If you put electricity into a quartz crystal you get movement, vibration, out. That is how all quartz watches work! So there is good reason to feel that the vibratory and electromagnetic properties of the human energy field, when conjoined with a suitable quartz crystal, can set up a resonant effect that can, in effect, create a protective energy shield.

To learn more visit www.stoneage.co.uk they have an amazing showroom in Glastonbury, England and the owner Lui Krieg will be happy to advise you.

The <u>Q-link pendant</u> is modern technology that uses a coil and compact self-powered circuitry to stabilise and strengthen your bodymind's energy field within the frequencies that occur in nature. Q-Link is actually the result of over 20 years of extensive research at top scientific institutions including Stanford University, Imperial College London and the University of Vienna. Research published in medical journals includes EEG Brain Wave Studies, Cellular Studies on Blood and Stress Tolerance of Human Tissue Cells.

How this actually works is not easy to explain but the Q-Link uses SRT (Sympathetic Resonance Technology) which integrates the biological and energetic functions of the body. It works along the same principles as acupuncture - but without the needles! Whenever you are under stress the first thing that is compromised is your bodymind's energetic system. If the stress continues then physical symptoms will occur such as headaches or mood swings, or maybe poor sleep. By continually helping the body to re-balance itself the Q-Link helps the wearer to simply run their body in a more efficient way. The Q-Link helps the energetic system of your body "correct itself". I wear the titanium one and it works for me. To find out more use an internet search engine or visit www.qlink-online. co.uk .

The use of teslar coil technology has been an interesting development. I have worn a special watch from Philip Stein, that houses two Teslar coils and they directly impart a beneficial electromagnetic pulse into your wrist. From there it travels throughout your body and, in my experience, it does have an effect. I had a wonderfully stimulating discussion with the inventor a few years ago who was genuinely surprised and delighted to meet someone who knew so much about the science and theory behind it. I was equally pleased by our discussions and saw a real niche for this product. The watch design is very clever because the power for the coils is what is used to actually power the watch movement as well. You can find out more about the fabulous looking and interesting Philip Stein watches and the resonance theory behind the Teslar coils at www. philipstein.com

TAKE A QUICK REFRESHER

In truth we own nothing but we are the custodians of much. We are each the appointed caretakers of all that is. We have not inherited this world from our ancestors; we have borrowed it from our descendants.
Wandering Star

Okay we have got this far on our journey. Hopefully it hasn't been too taxing! Now would be a good place to step aside and have a quick look at what we have covered so far. I have kept this simple. Here is a list of points for you to refresh your memory, confirm your understanding and also open you up to ideas or conclusions you might have at this stage.

- I wrote this book for YOU. I wrote it to share with you the keys to the incredible power you have to create and master your own destiny.
- Everything in your life comes to you through the Law of Attraction in response to your dominant thoughts and vibrations.
- Everything unfolds by the laws of cause and effect (karma). There is no "time out" from cause and effect. Even doing nothing is a cause that will have an effect.
- You are ultimately responsible for the circumstances, the effects, in your life
- It is no good looking around and to others for the key to your best life. It is within you – always.
- If you are not moving towards what you want, you are moving away from it.
- Your greatest opponent in getting what you want is your own negative programming.
- Think! Most people don't. If people were saying what they were thinking most of them would either be speechless or having arguments!
- The only time and place to be if you want to get a better life is HERE, NOW!
- The SELF Service Universe (SSU) has unlimited potential to respond to your dominant thoughts and intent, whether positive or negative.
- The technique for ordering what you want from the SSU is to decide what you want, ask for it, know it is yours already and receive it.
- The SSU is impartial and will deliver whatever you have ordered, good or bad.

- The real, eternal you is your Spiritually Existing Love Form, your SELF. Your SELF manifests in to the 4D universe as an energy field that drives your body.
- You are an energy field that has a body, not a body that has an energy field.
- Looking at things the other way round, often reveals that what first appears a 'problem' is usually an opportunity in disguise. Start to look at things differently seeking the opportunities rather than the problems.
- Your body is your vehicle, get a wellness check and keep it well serviced
- Most people are positively wishing but negatively thinking. The results are that they usually get what they don't want rather that what they do.
- Interesting times are there to divert and distract us from our purpose and mission here in the 4D. Don't get caught up in the illusions.
- Survival and wellness are not the same thing.
- Your mission is to become FREE and reconnect with your true SELF.
- It takes few words to speak truth.
- Feelings, even negative ones, can be a strong call to action. You can use anger to increase your range of action.
- It's better to take the plank out of your own eye before attempting to take the splinter out of the eye of someone else.
- It is not just the right of humans to be FREE but also for all sentient beings and life forms each to their own potentials. We are all connected to this world, to the web of life. In harming our planet we harm all living things and ourselves.
- Much of what you consider to be your thoughts and attitudes are in fact programmes installed by others such as parents, teachers, religion, politics etc.
- You don't run the programmes; they run you, often below your consciousness.
- Thoughts make things but your programmes often see that those things are not what you actually wanted. What a person thinks affects reality here in the physical universe.

- Your Spiritually Existing Love Form is the true driver of the bodymind vehicle.
- Your SELF is the immortal and eternal spark of spirit that chose to be in the classroom of physical human existence in order to take the curriculum and eventually graduate.
- Our brains offer almost limitless potential and processing power of which we use such a tiny amount. Decide to develop yourself and learn new skills and use more brain potential every day.
- Decisions are vital. Making a decision means cutting yourself off from any other course of action. Learn to appreciate the power of decisions and become an effective decision-maker.
- Every thought has a shape, that shape has a sound, that sound has a word and that word has power. Wisdom has been preserved and transmitted for thousands of years through stories.
- The media can put bias on events to reinforce certain programmes inside people's heads and therefore influence their behaviour.
- Most people continually sabotage their own lives because their programmes are undetected and allowed to undo their positive wishing through negative thinking.
- There is much more to biological life than literally meets the eye. All life evolves and exists within individual and collective electromagnetic fields of varying strengths, frequencies and range.
- There is a dense man-made electromagnetic fog that envelops the globe today.
- The DNA structures of biological life are not designed to operate in the artificial electromagnetic fields and microwave radiation now penetrating and surrounding the Earth today. At the fundamental level of this physical 4D universe DNA structures ARE energy fields.
- Our ancient ancestors built pyramids, temples and other sacred architecture as a means of enhancing important energy fields.
- We did not inherit this world from our forefathers; we are custodians of it for our descendants.
- The world is now seriously contaminated electromagnetically and chemically. You can do things to lessen the detrimental effects of the electromagnetic fog now surrounding and penetrating your physical

form.

- Wellness is a state of good mental, physical and spiritual health, supported and maintained by proper diet, exercise and beneficial habits. Wellness is when our Bodymind & Spirit are free from suffering allowing us to have the time, energy and freedom to live the life we want.
- Get a clear idea of where you need to make improvements in your nutrition, exercise, hygiene, mental processes and spirituality.
- There is currently not a clear line of communication from your SELF through to your 4D bodymind.
- Your SELF needs your physical bodymind vehicle, so look after it.
- Many of the illusions that have kept you 'comfortable' will begin to take on new appearances and natures that will not please you once you break away from the programmes that have been concealing things from you.
- Make a commitment to your SELF that you will become free and realise your true nature and potential.
- Do what you have always done and get what you always got or choose to change yourself NOW and thus change your circumstances.
- You might be the world's greatest yak herder, but until you climb a mountain and herd yaks you'll never know!

THINKING THE UNTHINKABLE?

The Great Spirit is in all things. He is in the air we breathe. The Great Spirit is our Father, but the Earth is our Mother. She nourishes us. That which we put in the ground She returns to us. Big Thunder (Bedagi) Wabanaki Algonquin

Most of us, as we learned earlier, have a brain equipped with billions of neuronal connections and quantum processors. The ability for these to produce an almost limitless information storage and retrieval capacity is well accepted. In theory there should be no limitations to what we can learn and remember. There should not be any real upper limits on our imagination and reasoning skills. However there is clear enough evidence that on average humanity is using only the tiniest fraction of the brain's potential in daily life. Just think what a waste and what a pity this is.

I have always held the simple view that I was unlimited in what I can do with my physical hard drive and its associated systems. Once I understood how I had acquired foreign installations, implanted limiting programmes, on my journey through the formative years of my life I decided to wipe them out. I did and in the process, I accessed my true SELF. The results have and will continue to be that I really do have an amazing life and a CV that reads like that of someone who is either impossibly old or is a modern Leonardo Da Vinci. In fact Leonardo was a hero of mine in my earlier years and I thought that he was only just scratching the surface of what a human is capable of. He was a scientist, artist, musician, alchemist, strategist, inventor, writer, philosopher, theologian and much more. So am I. The simple truth is that anyone can be multi-skilled if they work at it.

You should be aware of your massive potential. You should consider how much happier, healthier and wealthier you could be if you made even only a slight improvement and increase in the way you used your brain and your SELF. Certainly the SELF Service Universe doesn't see any difference between you and Leonardo Da Vinci. No, the SELF Service Universe is, as I have already indicated several times, operating to law and it is totally impartial and impersonal. Anything anyone else you admire has, you can have too. Anything anyone you look up to has achieved is there for you to achieve to.

To get what you want it is time for you to stretch your mind and flex those personal power 'fingers' in preparation of placing an order. An order that is a positive wish and that isn't sabotaged by negative thought or programming. Then you will start to get the things you want and avoid getting the things you don't want. What a difference that can make to your life. You can do this. So get start thinking new thoughts and stretching your mental faculties to get that brain of yours going!

As part of that process I'd like to expose you to something new right now. This is a train of thought and visualisation that literally is out of this world and I'd like to share it with you.

Consider the physical Universe that contains our world, solar system, our galaxy and countless other galaxies. This universe may be infinite or it may have boundaries but, as someone once observed, whatever its actual size it is really BIG. It is always going to turn out to be bigger than the biggest thing you can think off and then there are still loads more of it! It is probably beyond our 4D mental capability to truly grasp this limitless immensity because infinity isn't something we come up against everyday. Infinity isn't currently wired into our hard drive as an accessible and understandable concept. But that shouldn't stop you thinking about infinity and testing your mental equipment's ability to deal with new and challenging concepts.

The point about something being infinite is that there is always more of it. The best way to get a hold of this is to consider whether numbers are infinite. Actually there's a short cut you can take to prove to yourself that there are infinite numbers available in human mathematics. Just think of the biggest number ever reached and simply add one. No matter how long or big the number is another number can always be added to it! In terms of the universe we happen to have our precious planet residing within – there's probably no actual physical boundaries or limits to it. Now when I was a small child visualising something without any ending or boundaries used to really put my mind into a meltdown. It was great exercise and unlocked much of my mental processing capability that could have otherwise been unrealised.

In thinking such thoughts I used to lie awake at night attempting to visualise the vast reaches of the universe but somehow I always gave it edges. What was "outside" the universe though? Okay, so then I would imagine that the universe was biggest box ever but I had to put something – even if it were nothing – outside it. Then the trouble really starts because what's outside the outside? To my young brain the infinity concept wasn't something I could easily grasp. As for getting to grips with "nothing", not vacuum, not void but actual nothingness so no size, shape or time, well, you get the idea.

However I soon found ways around the problem of avoiding having edges or boundaries. What if the universe and all reality were somehow twisted into an interesting endless loop. It would have to quite some twisting because it would have to be uniformly warped in all directions. That was okay with this young mind because if everything were twisted uniformly through all dimensions none of us would ever know it was otherwise. What we see as a straight line could well be something else but it and the sensory equipment seeing it were operating within the warped structure as part of the 'twisting' too!

I considered such a universal structure as a candidate for testing the way to have a boundary-less universe. Bear with me here, I was only about 8 years old at the time. So, I then needed to test this out and imagined having the most powerful telescope in the universe available (hey, I was a kid I could have anything inside my head) and a temporal field accelerator to overcome the limitations of light speed. That way I would overcome the need to wait billions upon billions of years for light to reach me. With this 'in mind' I imagined looking straight-ahead through the telescope and thought I would, at the farthest distance of the universe, be looking at the back of my head irrespective of what direction I looked!

Now with the latest thinking in science with regard to the structure, the coherence of the universe and the missing 'dark' matter, I reckon I was onto something forty years ago! If any scientists out there are reading this book and fancy a chat that's great. So you can see how I stretched and tested my mental faculties from an early age. Over time this activity and thought processes expanded my mental abilities well beyond what they would otherwise have been. In my life I have turned my attention to many things and have done more in the past thirty or so years than most will do in lifetimes. To me there are now always possibilities and yes, I just might be the world's greatest yak herder. This infinite universe idea makes that and so much more possible for me.

Look at it from my perspective for a moment. If the universe truly is infinite then it can contain an infinite number of possibilities. No matter what you can imagine there's every chance that sometime, somewhere, it has manifest. When you have infinite space and time available then even the biggest thing is, compared with infinity, relatively microscopic. It also follows that even the longest spans of time are but a twinkling of an eye.

I am older now but I still enjoy challenging myself with new ideas and concepts. Over the years I have truly come to love like the idea of infinite possibilities and infinite diversity. What the quantum physicist might call the probability amplitude awaiting collapse of the wave function is a magical recipe for manifesting some fascinating concepts. With this in mind I invite you to come along now to an incredibly distant part of the universe a very, very long time ago.

An incredibly long time ago in galaxies far, far away there was a problem. Now problems are always popping in and out of existence in an infinite universe. On the whole, with infinity of time on hand even a huge problem will eventually be seen as a mere trifle. But this problem had been hanging around for so long those life forms it concerned had just about given up hoping to find a solution. These beings were huge sentient fields of energy many thousands of miles across that could change size, shape and density at will. For the sake of this tale I will call these beings Ergons.

The Ergons had existed for millions of years and, in that time, had travelled mind-boggling distances throughout the universe. They had swum in the nuclear fires of giant stars, danced around black holes, 'walked' upon countless worlds, observed various civilisations and forms of life, and studied everything. The human brain with its billions of neurons has an almost limitless capacity to handle and store knowledge, so we can hardly imagine what data millions of cubic miles of organised intelligent energy can accumulate.

That was the start of the problem. One by one the Ergons became aware of a simple fact: there was nothing NEW in their existence. They had seen all, heard all, sensed all and memorised all the stimuli their incredibly long lifespan had experienced. You could say they were the universe's biggest know-alls! An Ergon could travel vast distances, arrive at a galaxy and instantly know the location, composition and state of everything it contained.

Some Ergons tried to alleviate boredom by experimenting with various life forms – sometimes entire civilisations – but their knowledge and ability to calculate the outcomes spoilt all the fun!

No Ergon had been 'born' or had 'died' in millions of years and the prospect of eternal boredom was all too real too terrible to contemplate. Knowing they were immortal there was no sure way to 'die' and thus escape. A solution was required.

It was one of the 'youngest' that finally came up with the radical solution. The idea was incredible: why not scatter and then all converge simultaneously on the same point in space-time at light speed? Better still why not bring all the stars and matter they could gather along too? The result would go beyond even the largest black hole ever detected and the millisecond after they all fused together there would be a glorious bang like the universe had never witnessed.

The plan was unanimously accepted and carried out exactly as planned. The Ergons all converged on the same space-time co-ordinates and there was a bang. It was a very BIG BANG, the biggest bang ever. As energy beings the Ergons didn't cease to exist but rather became fragments scattered throughout the vastness of the new universe they had just created. Fused with star stuff and energy fields the immortal Ergon sparks, too many to count, began to re-experience life in the universe. Each spark carried a different and unique 'bit' of an original Ergon's knowledge and personality.

And so they lived, and died, and lived, and died in a cycle of never-ending re-birth throughout the universe. Now changed forever as immortal sparks encased in form seeking to explore and re-discover the secrets they once knew. Driven by a desire to have adventures in the realms of space-time and the spiritual dimensions they manifest themselves as sentient beings on worlds throughout the universe. Inside them they hold a burning desire to belong, to interconnect with each other and to understand their existence. So even now they journey on in their post big bang adventures.

That's the story of the Ergons and their ultimate solution. If a story is all that it is to you I hope you enjoyed it. If, however, you feel it makes a kind of sense then it can be quite a comfort! If you ever have one of those quiet moments of feeling alone and separate, moments of longing to 'find' a soul mate or to 'belong', or feel a sense of a bigger picture somehow just beyond your memory's reach – don't worry about it too much. Just remember the story of the Ergons!

Some pointers:
- Our brains have almost unlimited capacity for data processing and unlimited potential.
- Humanity is using only the tiniest fraction of the brain's potential in daily life.
- Stretch and expand your mental capabilities by exposing yourself to new things.
- If the universe is infinite then it can contain an infinite number of possibilities.

NOTES, IDEAS AND SCRIBBLES

THE SOUND OF SILENCE
"If a tree falls in the forest when there is no one around to hear it, does it make any sound?"

Zen Koan

Getting back to the whole issue of your true nature and potential, here, in a nutshell, is the fundamental problem that needs attention. Your SELF is having communication problems and cannot be heard because of all the "noise" that your bodymind is producing.

You are "talking" mentally to yourself most of the time at hundreds of words a minute. Sometimes you are flattering yourself, other times you are kicking yourself and putting yourself down. Often you are simply maintaining a dialogue that keeps you within the "comfort zone" of who you believe yourself to be. Most of that "self chatter" is programmed material absorbed from family, friends, religious upbringing, educational experience and so on. Sometimes it makes sense and yet sometimes it seems to be just irritating bits of songs, phrases and self-talk by your ego.

This mental background dialogue is something we need to be aware of and work towards gaining control of it. The mental chattering is the culprit responsible for turning your positive wishing into negative thinking. That way you don't get what you wished for and you wonder why. So through the act of witnessing our thoughts as a conscious process and through stilling the bodymind with meditation we are going to back up your positive wishing with powerful, results generating positive thinking.

Many people only really notice this bodymind noisiness when they're lying in bed trying to sleep and that mental racket just won't shut up! I have sympathy because I've been there myself. But that's not good enough. Becoming free and in control of your power to create your destiny absolutely requires that you have your thought processes entirely on your side. We are going to learn the techniques that allow us to watch and listen to our thoughts in action.

But just consider something. If it is <u>you</u> that is doing all the mental chattering, then who is it that's doing the listening? More to the point, when I ask you to pay attention to this bodymind "noise" - just to get aware of it - who is it that is observing the one who is listening to the one who is doing all that chattering? There must be a fair lot of "you" in there. What are you all doing and which, if any, is the true non-illusory you?

That's a bit of a tricky one but I think you can admit that you can hear your internal thoughts when you pay attention. You can also observe yourself listening to your thoughts and see how they hook you and drag you along. So once again I must ask; who are you, or more importantly which one is you?

You cannot fully explore these and similar questions whilst dealing with the background din of mental self-talk and programmed responses. You are generating too much mental static to be able to sustain a clean connection to the energy field of universal intelligence residing in and through all that you recognise as the universe and its contents. Without a clear channel the soft signals that come from your true being go unheard, or rather unperceived. If you cannot possibly hear your true SELF then you are unable to enter into the dialogue you need with your inner knowing. If you cannot hear your SELF you are unlikely to recognise it for what it is when it does get through. From time to time even the noisiest mind stalls and the small voice of the SELF gets its chance to attempt to tell you something. Sadly it can go unrecognised or written off – because it appears 'different' – as just your imagination or mind playing tricks.

I know that sometimes it is easier to just tell yourself that it is imagination.

But your small quiet voice of SELF exists. It is an extrusion of vibrations from a universal (all encompassing) energy field which exists at the smallest possible scale of detection. Many leading scientists and philosophers have explored the strange realm of quantum mechanics and found this field to be the best description for what manifests at the realm below atoms and their constituent 'particles'. It has been likened to quantum foam and also is being hailed as the unifier for a superstring theory. The field is everywhere and it has, not surprisingly, many names. Amongst some currently in use it is called variously "the force" or the "zero point field" or the "unified field" and it is the key, so science hopes, to the long awaited Theory Of Everything (TOE). The

TOE notwithstanding, this field is best imagined as an all-encompassing sea of energy with unlimited potentials and possibilities bubbling about. It contains data of everything that is, has been and can be. It includes the intelligence and awareness of many life forms that may, or may not, currently manifest as a physical form. So if you can establish a link with the field and interpret the data well enough, you can gain knowledge and information that was downloaded from the consciousness of those who are no longer in body.

Let us get back to the struggle for the SELF to make itself heard. Your mind is full of all sorts of self-talk and playbacks. I think you realise that in all fairness it's pretty noisy in there. I often hear people saying they can't hear themselves think. What they recognise is that there's too much 'stuff' in their head that they can't focus on the matter that is most pressing.

We have to find a way to shut off all the noise and dispose of a lot of the 'stuff' that doesn't serve in getting you and your SELF together.

That silence and stillness will calm and relax the bodymind, help release stress and allow the first whisperings of your true SELF to be heard. It is a small, quiet voice and, once you hear it, you understand how it couldn't possibly compete with the incredibly loud sounds of your ego. This voice will help you to learn and to listen. You will also be allowing your bodymind to do what it can to keep up with the demands of this physical realm.

The best method for achieving that stillness is for you to develop your ability to meditate. Now don't jump to any conclusions just yet. I realise that meditation is often misunderstood and has been hijacked once or twice by various groups and sects.

However, when you cut away all the hype and dogma, meditation is the simple process of calming the bodymind. It is not about focus or imagination although they can have a role in your mental life later if you so choose. But to get the communication channel to the SELF open and clear initially requires a state of no-mind to be achieved. In doing this you gain the meditative state, you empower the biological intelligence to get on with essential repairs and maintenance, improve your personal wellness, plus the SELF gets the opportunity to be heard. So, meditation has the potential to deliver health benefits as well as mental and spiritual ones.

A few key points from this chapter:

- Your SELF is having communication problems tuning in to your 4D physical manifestation.
- You are "talking" mentally to yourself most of the time at hundreds of words a minute. A lot of this can be negative and therefore limiting you.
- If you cannot hear your SELF you are unlikely to recognise it when it does get through.
- Everything that "exists" – or rather everything that we perceive to have existence - is an extrusion of vibrations from a universal (all encompassing) energy field which exists at the smallest possible scale of detection.
- You can still the bodymind and lessen the mental chatter through meditation.

SAY HELLO TO THE BODYMIND

Grant yourself a moment of peace and you will understand how foolishly you have scurried about. Learn to be silent and you will notice that you have talked too much. Be kind and you will realise that your judgement of others was too severe. Tschen Tschi Ju

I have used a term several times, which you have noticed but may not have understood. The term is "bodymind" and it is a very important one. For a long time philosophy, religion and medicine have employed a basic approach of separating the body that is the physical, from the mind. But they are inter-linked at a fundamental level. You may well have heard of psychosomatic disorders. The term is made up of "psycho", the mind or mental - and "soma", the body or physical. I used this word earlier. The term psychosomatic was coined to account for the phenomenon of something mental in origin having a demonstrable effect on the body.

People who regularly imagine that they are ill best demonstrate this. They are called hypochondriacs and they can manifest all the symptoms of their imagined illness. In a real sense they actually are ill. They show the powerful inter-linking of the mental and physical in their psychosomatic disorders. It is also the same mechanism acting in a positive way that allows the 'placebo effect' to operate. That's where a patient is given medicine for a condition under the impression that is an accepted curative. In fact the tablet or injection is harmless sugar or saline. The patient is unaware of this and proceeds to get better thanks to the 'medicine' they have been given. The bodymind has accepted the illusion and acted as though it is reality.

If your mind is ill or damaged you go to an analyst, psychologist or psychiatrist to get things "fixed". If your body is damaged or ill you go to a physician or surgeon for physical treatment. If both are in a mess you have double the trouble getting it sorted! The being who became 'The Buddha' clearly perceived and understood the problem as he sat beneath a tree seeking the solution to man's entrapment in suffering. You will read about Buddha later in a story that is part of this teaching. He left us a wonderful gift through explaining his understanding of a powerful truth. Understanding that the body and mind were not two but one, Buddha gave us the "bodymind" as a single entity. He had realised that mental suffering and illusions were echoed in, and affected, the physical aspect of the bodymind. Equally he understood that bodily suffering was echoed in, and influenced, the mental aspect of the bodymind.

Science, medicine and religion have, for the most part, overlooked the bodymind. Holistic medicine and various complementary therapies have begun to rediscover this basic truth, understanding that circulation, breathing, muscle tone and metabolism are all affected by one's mental state. When you experience fear or panic your breathing, heartbeat, body chemistry and muscle tone are all altered. The effects can be so obvious that they take a while to wear off afterwards. Most of us have at least some memory of having felt the physical effects of a frightening event. Even if the fear is purely imaginary, the bodymind's reaction is just as real. You only have to wake up from a nightmare to test the truth of it!

Consider someone who is very uncomfortable with heights watching a movie of someone hanging precariously over the edge of a mountain and falling. They know it is just a movie. They are not more than a couple of feet off the ground at the time but guess what? Their hands shake and the palms become slick with sweat. Their heart is racing and their breathing speeds up. Now tell me that your mental events don't affect your physical ones!

The bodymind is attached to so many desires, feelings and appetites. The ego is also attached to so many beliefs, wants, needs and the body it "inhabits". By stilling and silencing the mind aspect the body aspect follows suit and vice versa. Somehow, Buddha reasoned, he needed to find a way to deal with the bodymind simply so that what lay behind it could be revealed.

So he set out to discover and perfect the means of stilling the bodymind and removing the distractions and afflictions that were the nature of so-called physical "reality". The challenge was that these illusions, afflictions and distractions are moving targets. Every time you become aware of them something else pops up long enough for everything to move quickly out of the spotlight. But Buddha realised that the trick was to observe but not get hooked by such things. Having then achieved this through the use of meditation he was then free to observe the illusions and attachments that had held him up to that point.

Several years spent living in the forest with a group of ascetics and punishing his body with harsh yogic practices and poor diet hadn't freed him. But now, with the clarity that arose out of a stilled and silent bodymind, he saw the ego and the myth of a separate physical "self". He knew the illusion of the separate "self" was manifesting through the ego and all its associated programmes. This separate self had taken control and seized the power that belonged to the true being, that which was part of the true SELF. The illusory nature of reality, in being accepted by the egoic self, creates the possibility of attachment and suffering. The principle cause of human suffering as far as Buddha was concerned, was this process of grasping, of forming attachments to the impermanent and illusory world, in placing our happiness and awareness at the mercy of things outside of us. As long as either body or ego held sway over any individual, then the ability for that being to break the attachments and pierce the illusions to become *free* was simply not present.

His observations had revealed that the ego, the false self, would not be shut down easily. It would fight to avoid being silenced and would use all the resources of the bodymind and its attachments to the external to distract the seeker from their objective. But the method he perfected was the key and, by diligent application, he knew it worked.

If he could achieve this by himself, then he could refine the techniques and pass them on to the world at large. His method would cause the inner being of the true SELF to be liberated and empowered to use the bodymind as a tool to experience and interact with the universe. The ego might remain in some form, but it would be far less powerful by being known and recognised for what it was. Never again would its web of illusion and negativity hold back the true seeker from their journey back to their source. By seeing that all that was external to the SELF was impermanent and also seeing that the ego, the false self, had created many attachments and had been grasping at illusions, the seeker could at last become free.

This understanding of how the human ego generates unhappiness as it grasps at 'things' outside of itself and, through these attachments creates limitations, mental phenomena and suffering is a jewel of great price for those who find it. We must recognise that many people will argue strongly that they are already happy. Indeed some will really believe that they have never had it so good. Those who cling to the illusions of material existence are in for some unpleasant shocks as the 21st century progresses.

However, it is necessary to be focussed in our mission and we choose to honour another's choice to argue for their limitations or defend their intrinsic unhappiness. There are none so blind as those who will not see, and none so deaf as those who will not hear. You have to resist the wasteful use of your energy and personal power that arises when you attempt to 'convert' or assist those who will have none of it. Impeccability is a quality that all with personal power derived from reconnecting to their true nature and SELF prize highly. By impeccability I mean the application of one's energy and effort without error or deviation.

I am amazed at how often people make more effort to dismiss a new and interesting concept or possibility, than it would take for them to embrace and experiment with it. As I mentioned earlier, I have discovered that people have a tendency to quit when they are nearer to success than to failure in any endeavour. That is simply a waste of energy and effort arising from the negativity of their egos and programmes.

We will pay attention to the people who are prepared to make an effort to improve their lives and circumstances by exercising an open mind and heart. By accepting that there are always possibilities that we have not encountered before, we open ourselves to the wonders of the universe. There are plenty of people who are currently in a state of fear, anxiety, delusion or depression who will readily acknowledge this and, on this basis, they need our help. Their primary causes for unhappiness and suffering through attachment and acceptance of illusions will vary but we can certainly predict that the main factors will be:

Financial: so many people are under pressure and probably in debt. In this modern world people drive themselves even harder just to stay "afloat". Many of them suffer as they realise they are just treading water financially whilst the banks and big organisations patiently wait for them to tire and drown. Misery is a big business these days.

Health: I see so many people around me with worries about their health or dissatisfaction with their current well being. Disabilities and addictions account for a great deal of unhappiness to those directly concerned – which includes family, friends and carers.

Environmental: there are certainly more and more people becoming aware of the environmental impacts of modern living and wanting to change things or "do their bit" for the environment. However, they find many reasons and justifications as to why they are helpless to make any difference on their own. The failure is to realise that every worthwhile cause that ever came into being in human history started with an individual. It truly only takes one to begin anything but most of us want that 'one' to be someone else first!

Spiritual: so many people are feeling challenged and even lost in this supposed 'new age" where there is overload of 'spiritual guidance & techniques" but no clear way ahead. The spiritual challenge is the clear indication that people are not in their power. Even if they adopt a particular spiritual practise they soon begin to feel that things are not improving enough and so they move on looking for the next 'answer'. The problem is still the positive wishing being sabotaged by the negative thinking embedded in the programmes they are running.   Only by reinforcing their genuine positive desires with the full power of positive thinking can they begin to manifest what they seek.

Lifestyle: well this is so obvious when I look around. I see square pegs in round holes, exploited employees, frustrated entrepreneurs, the undervalued and the displaced persons all wondering what life is about and what they should be doing differently. Well the answer is here in this simple guide. By reconnecting to their true inner being, bypassing the ego and false self and disengaging the negative programming they can make changes for the lifestyle they truly want.

Emotional: Damaged and failing relationships and low self-esteem are two key factors at work on the emotional level. Also a deep inner sense that things are not the way they are supposed to be creates emotional reactions of loneliness and alienation. The feeling that most humans have that they are 'separate' is a powerful illusion. Only by stilling the bodymind and accessing the true and eternal spark of the SELF can we experience the simple fact that all things are connected. The web of creation, the interlinking cause and effect of interdependent reality makes it impossible for anything, to be separate and totally isolated from creation.

These are just simple brush strokes, but they clearly indicate the immensity of the challenges that face those of us who have already established a connection to our true nature and power. There are many difficulties and great rewards to be experienced in assisting people in all these categories – and in others we have not yet identified.

Some points from this chapter:
- Philosophy, religion and medicine have employed a basic approach of separating the body, that is the physical, from the mind. But they are inter-linked at a fundamental level.
- The body and mind are not two but one that is the bodymind.
- Mental suffering and illusions affect the physical aspect of the bodymind. Equally bodily suffering influences the mental aspect of the bodymind.
- Even if the fear is purely imaginary, the bodymind's reaction to it is real.
- Buddha observed that the ego, the false self, would not be shut down easily and would keep one from becoming free.
- Stilling the bodymind is the key to unlocking the ego's hold and seeing past our programming.
- Human ego generates unhappiness as it uses programmes to make us grasp at 'things' outside of itself and, through these attachments creates limitations and suffering.
- There are none so blind as those who will not see, and none so deaf as those who will not hear.
- People tend to quit when they are nearer to success than to failure.

NOTES, IDEAS AND SCRIBBLES

A MEDITATION NOT TO BE MYTHED

"Empty yourself of everything. Let the mind be still. The ten thousand things rise and fall while the Self watches their return. They grow and flourish and then return to the source. Returning to the source is stillness, which is the way of nature." Lao Tsu

The simple bet effective method of stilling the bodymind discovered by Buddha was what we call meditation. The beauty of the meditation method developed by Buddha was in its very simplicity. It also had the excellent merit of actually working! With diligent practise anyone could become a proficient meditator and gain the opportunity to be liberated from the myths of their egos and their illusory reality. All they had to do was keep it simple and be true to the method.

That's the snag! Simplicity sounds easy enough but a little thought and experience of our daily lives will tell us we rarely achieve it. We have learned to complicate things. We like to add a little myth, mystery and hype. Our ego takes anything simple and complicates it. It breaks it down into little pieces, shuffling them around until a jigsaw puzzle remains. The ego then spends more time and energy reconstructing the picture, adding a bit here, removing or losing pieces there, until the thing is finally "solved". Then it goes on to something else and does it all over again. Most people are so caught up in this method of complication that they actually enjoy it. They don't recognise it as distraction at all. In fact I have, on more occasions than I care to remember, heard "it can't be that simple!" exclaimed in a wide range of situations where, quite frankly, it was.

The key to the particular meditation devised by Buddha is that it *is* simple. You need to be aware that you'll certainly be tempted to complicate it. That is because, by now, your ego knows what we are up to. It will not accept that anything could be so simple. There will be no satisfaction for the ego in having you spending time and energy on mastering the necessary inaction and simplicity. It wants frantic rushing around, lots of mental chatter and as much complication as can possibly be created. Follow the method as given by Buddha and your ego certainly won't be getting any of that.

Be assured that your ego cannot make it complicated if you follow the method as given to you and keep on meditating whenever you can. Use no frills, no fancy tricks, just use the simple and pure method. It's child's play and that is its real power. Because, for nearly nine months (on average) you were in a continual state that is the one this meditation is designed to restore to you.

Once upon a time you were floating in the dark with only the heartbeat and breathing as your constant companions in your mother's womb. Your bodymind was left to get on with its allotted tasks. It spent those nine months building the body you were born with from a small clump of cells. Meanwhile the driver, the true you as an extension of your eternal SELF was simply being.

Once you were born your SELF then embarked on a journey to master that vehicle as a device for movement, sight, sound, touch, smell and taste within this physical universe. It imprinted a version of itself within your physical form to take charge and this aspect of your Spiritual Existing Love Form became the 'You'. You learned to co-ordinate and run the bio-computer and then, somewhere along the way, it began to run you. It runs you with the programmes that were installed by external factors and authorities. That's how the other yous arrived, as artificial selves we know as the ego.

Now, through this process we are investigating you are beginning a new journey back to the driving seat and reclaiming the vehicle as your own. On the way you will need to uninstall a lot of programmes that you will identify as parasites that do not serve you or your SELF. You will also need to unlearn some strong habits that have held you back from your true SELF and potential.

The starting point for understanding how these programmes and thought habits have taken over is by learning to detach that aspect, that 'you' that was installed by your SELF as the original and rightful ruler of your physical form and life. By detaching you can then learn to observe these programmes and habits, without getting caught up and carried of by them. The technique for this learning experience is meditation and awareness. Like all things in this polarised universe there are two sides or opposites involved. This means that we begin by stilling the bodymind through meditation and detachment but we will also need to cultivate the opposite condition, which is 'mindfulness'. For now we need to take the first steps towards a better understanding and that is through meditation.

The meditation we are going to use for stilling the bodymind, as developed by Buddha, is commonly called Vipassna which is a word in the Pali tongue that comes originally from the Sanskrit word Vippassyanna. You've probably heard of it before and, happily, it is growing in popularity at a time when the world really needs the benefits of a stilled bodymind. The word Vippassyanna means, "to look". That is the literal translation. However, the metaphorical meaning is better understood as "to watch" or "to witness". We will explore this meaning further and get acquainted with the simplicity of the method itself. Firstly, however, I need to deal with the bewildering array of meditational techniques that are springing up all over the place.

Now let's be clear about this, I have nothing against guided meditations, creative visualisation meditations and other such practises. But they should be an activity you choose because they're appropriate for the purpose. Maybe you'll experiment with them out of simple curiousity. That's fine and I'm sure you'll get something out of it all. What you won't get if you start out this way is the freedom from your ego and programmes that you need. That's because engaging in these other meditational techniques before you've attained and integrated the benefits of Vipassna means that the "journeys" you make are almost certainly generated by the ego's programmes and imagination.

You see what is vital in any such activity as the Celestine, Pleiadean, Goddess or other such guided meditation is the departure point. Where you are when you launch into these is of great importance and relevance. Don't, by the way, misunderstand me, I have experienced a variety of different meditations and they can wonderful tools. They are great provided the meditator has learned to identify and disengage the trickster that is the ego.

If your departure point isn't from your true being then, in truth, you're not going anywhere. Whatever you experience no matter how "real" it seems it is a construct of your ego's access to imagination and memory. If you want to escape the bonds of the physical 4D universe you have to have mastered the bodymind and then your departure point is a truly powerful launching pad into the infinite.

So I suggest that you take Vipassna as the essential starting point and, once you get that working for you, look forward to all the other possibilities with the confidence that of knowing who and what you really are. Vipassna meditation is, as we've already learned, a method for watching and witnessing. The object of that witnessing is something that is a constant phenomenon in you and everyone around you. It is the *breath*. The simple instruction on witnessing the breath that I write here, allied to your diligent practice, will be more than enough for your needs. It just depends on your ability, at this point in your development, to avoid complicating it.

Firstly, let me free you of a basic misconception about posture. You don't need to adopt the lotus posture for meditation if it is a position alien to you. The lotus posture (sitting on the ground, legs crossed, feet crossed over and hands in your lap) was developed by people who didn't have or use chairs and had sat that way all their lives. For those used to chairs it can, at first, be a difficult and uncomfortable position. You don't need it to be a meditator. As far as your posture is concerned you only need to be sure that your spine is as straight as possible, that you are not uncomfortable (no danger of "pins and needles" in your legs) and that you will not fall over! That's it. You can be seated in an armchair, leaning against a wall, or even reclining on cushions. People confined to bed can meditate just as effectively as any loose-limbed yoga adept!

You need to be somewhere that is not too warm or too cold because, particularly when first starting out in meditation, things can very easily distract you. The quieter the location you choose to meditate in the better the results can be. The method of Vipassna couldn't be any simpler. You position yourself with your spine as straight as you can. Make your body comfortable and safe with your eyes closed. Then you simply _witness your body breathing._

In that last sentence you have the whole thing in its total simplicity. Don't complicate it. Go back over that sentence again and make certain you remember it – exactly.

Once you are sitting comfortably with your eyes closed, you focus your attention on the breath as it enters and leaves your body through your nose. The point of attention as a watcher or witness is the nostrils. Now that sounds very simple - but I happen to know that it isn't easy! That's because to witness the breath doesn't mean *interfering or altering* it in any way. It must simply happen and be witnessed by you.

That is hard to start with because, for most people, breathing is automatic until they notice it. Then somehow the system switches to "manual" and you have to take over! I know because I've been there! It is infuriating at first but you have to "let go" and trust that, if left alone, the body will breathe for you - sooner rather than later!

There is no concentration and no thought. Just witness your breath coming in and going out. As you do so you will soon become aware of all kinds of mental "chatter" and stray thoughts arising. The trick is to ignore them and keep witnessing the breath. The mental "noise" only becomes really apparent when you meditate. This reveals an interesting paradox. If you are simply witnessing the breath coming in and going out of the body, and can observe these various thoughts arising in the otherwise silent space then who is doing the thinking? Who is doing the breathing? And who, after all that, is doing the witnessing?

THE PROUD ARCHER

Everything on the Earth has a purpose. Every disease has an herb to cure it. Every person has a mission. This is the Indian theory of existence. Morning Dove, Salish.

There was once a bright young lad, for this story I shall call him Simon. He was one of those people you sometimes come across who seem to be able to do just about anything they put their mind to. Such people tend to get distracted by their own abilities and the lure of so many new things to do. They tend to end up flitting from one thing to the next, only ever alighting long enough to say "I can do that!" before going after some newer more alluring bloom. (I call these people "butterflies" and this young man was exactly that.)

Now it just so happened that he lived in a decent sized village where there were many different arts, crafts and disciplines being pursued and so he had exposure to many different things. Naturally, he was pretty good at anything he tried and so he developed a very strong sense of superiority. Yes, Simon's broad range of abilities was equally matched by the broadness of his over-developed ego.

One day whilst in the farthest part of the village he came across a stranger who was just "passing through". This stranger was not particularly special to look at, but he did have a beautiful hunting bow and a quiver of arrows slung around his shoulders. These caught our young man's attention and interest because he hadn't seen a bow and arrow before. Well not close up and in the flesh! So, not lacking in confidence or a sense of his own importance in the village he approached the stranger and engaged him in a conversation.

"I've never had a chance to fire a bow and arrow before" he told the stranger.

"Haven't you now young lad?" the stranger was in a friendly mood it seemed. "Would you be interested in archery then?"

"Archery you say? Is that what it's called? Yes, I'd like very much to have a go at archery. I'm pretty good with a sword, a staff, a slingshot and, of course, I'm good with my fists too!" The youngster had no hesitation about bragging even to a complete stranger.

"Oh is that so? Are you good at everything you do then?" asked the stranger with a wry smile.

110

"Well" boasted our hero "I've not yet found something around here I couldn't do! My father says I'm going to make something of my life and be a wealthy and successful man."

The stranger smiled. To be fair to Simon, the youngster was actually quite likeable and, in his opinion, being cocky was a valid approach to life in hard times. The stranger decided that he would humour Simon and, who knows, maybe here was a potential champion. So the stranger took Simon outside the village into a field where, using an empty water barrel, he set up a target to aim at. After a quick demonstration of how to handle the bow and arrows, and some hints and guidance, Simon was ready to loose his first arrow at the poor unsuspecting water barrel. He pulled with all his might and drew back the bowstring to his cheek as he'd been shown. The bow was a mighty weapon built for the powerful stranger and so his muscles strained and his sinews creaked as he struggled to hold the tension. Then he let the arrow fly. It flew well and true and struck the barrel fully in the centre.

"Well done lad!" The stranger was impressed. "You look like a natural to me. You should get yourself a good bow made and practise what I've shown you. Then perhaps you might be able to come and enter the county's archery tournament in a couple of months and perhaps even win a purse of silver and some fame!"

Well, as you can imagine, that did it! Simon's father was pestered until a suitable bow and some arrows were provided. If you are a parent you will know how constant requests from your children wear down your original resolve to say no! Soon enough Simon had his desired bow and arrows and to be fair, for the first time the lad actually stuck at something. Every day he went to that field and practised shooting at the barrel. He never missed and could even do it with his eyes shut. That was a stunt which he used to impress several young ladies of the village and, before long, his prowess with the bow, arrows and barrel got him entered into the county archery tournament. The stranger had clearly known his stuff when he originally instructed Simon. Because it turned out that the target at the tournament was the same distance away and similar in size to the barrel back in the village field. So Simon won the contest easily. Even taking one turn with a blindfold on, which won him much acclaim!

In the crowd was a master archer who everyone paid due respect to.

Everyone that is, except Simon, who was full of pride. With his purse of silver in hand, he presented himself to the master whom, it has to be said, seemed remarkably unimpressed. However, the master agreed to take him into his school where he would train with other young archers who were seeking to perfect their skills.

For a few weeks Simon was the star of the school. As others struggled to hit the target, never mind the bright red bull's-eye, he was nonchalantly placing arrow after arrow back into the centre. But gradually they all caught up with him.

Then one day the master appeared and said, "Today we are going to attempt something different. Today we will be testing each of you and those who fail to hit the target an acceptable number of times will be leaving us."

All of the students fidgeted nervously. That is all of them except for our young hero who smiled cockily at the rest and said "Sure thing master." He then looked at his fellow students as if to say "So long, losers!"

What happened next? The master tied the target to the side of a mule cart, which raced backwards and forwards in front of the archers. Simon was totally thrown when, after taking aim and letting fly, he missed the target, and the cart, by several yards. The target simply wasn't where it was supposed to be! Once he'd sighted the thing, taken his aim and let fly, the target was somewhere else when the arrow got there. So Simon's performance was the worst of any student and, in obedience to the master's command, he was told to leave the school. Meanwhile the students he'd lorded over all passed the test easily and were therefore invited to stay with the master.

"That wasn't a fair test!" Simon protested to the master.

"Why wasn't it fair, my son?" asked the master (with it has to be said, a ghost of a smile on his face) "tell how you would have it otherwise?"

"Well" protested our fallen hero "the target couldn't be hit. It didn't keep still like the barrel or the bull's-eye did before! It wasn't a fair test because the target was always moving."

"Ah but that's precisely the point, my son" replied the master "you see in real life, the targets are always moving."

EXPLORING THIS STORY

Because Simon had been only experienced in shooting at a static target and hitting the bull's-eye every time, he thought to himself "Wow! Look at me I can really hit that target every time. I'm that good I can do it with my eyes shut!" Therefore if some other students come along and have difficulty in hitting that target Simon gains a feeling of superiority. Of course this supposed superiority is a programme, and therefore it is keeping him from accessing his true potential. This kind of superiority, or egoic programme is also designed to inflict inferiority on the others around him.

It is a pretty common enough kind of oppression, which is easily observed manifesting in many different ways and continually causing unhappiness around the world today. Just consider how many people maintain their so called 'authority' over others in the workplace, in private relationships, in government, simply by virtue of having developed a powerful sense of superiority that then causes other to feel inferior. You know exactly what I am talking about don't you?

But in this story one day things change and present our hero with the sensation of suddenly not being superior. This is a rude awakening that can trigger other programmes that have been idling in the hard drive of his brain. The target is now moving and this time, hitting the bull's-eye is actually the only thing that counts and our guy just can't get an arrow anywhere near the thing. What a shock! Can you imagine his flaunted superiority so spectacularly collapsing in full view of his supposed "inferiors"? What a blow to his huge ego and what a wonderful stimulus for self-realisation and change!

Sadly the common response to a deflated ego is one of anger and seeking to blame anything but the true culprit. But eventually we run out of things and people to blame and we are forced to consider our own responsibility for the outcomes we are getting. When Simon can't hit that moving target time after time he runs out of external factors to blame. Instead of *fixing the blame he then considers how to fix the problem.* That is a mature decision that already shows his potential for improving his situation. He realises that he's now going to have to unlearn and disempower the programmes that no longer serve him. So the whole process of becoming a great archer has to begin again. He has to unlearn

113

that which he thought was archery and to start from scratch and discover what archery is really about. He has to understand what the true nature of marksmanship really is, rather than the illusion he'd supported before.

He begins to make meaningful progress when he understands it's not about hitting a target you have deliberately made consistent and predictable in its space-time co-ordinates. He can now see beyond that programme and begin to realise that the true process of archery is about opening up his awareness. He drops his programmes about the targets conforming to his expectations and previous experience. He realises that he needs to simply be open to the infinity of possible targets. His true aim, as a marksman, is to achieve mindfulness and to be ready to identify whatever target finally manifests. Only then, when he can recognise and hit that bull's-eye irrespective of whether it is moving, is still, up a tree, on the back of a moving wagon, close to or far, can he understand archery.

We are all likely to find ourselves thrown by the position and movement of the targets in our daily lives. You sometimes might ask why it is that you keep seeing the same things coming around again and again. You may well ask! The answer is the same for you as it was for our young archer. Because you did it once, understood the explanation, recognised the demonstration, empowered it and integrated the principle it had to teach, doesn't mean this is the only way that principle, that lesson, will continue to manifest itself. The principle is the same. But the conditions and manifestations of the possible situations that principle can apply to are *many*. Whether you live to be fifty or five thousand years of age, still I can guarantee, even at that length of time that situations will occur where you will be taking aim for the very first time.

But if you are like the student archer you will now understand the true nature of archery as a process of aiming appropriately according to the situation and nature of the target. You will learn to discard any expectations, which lure you into a possible future and away from the now, where you need to be.

By being present without expectations or negative programmes running you begin to achieve the marksmanship necessary to hit any moving target in your life. You can begin to actually see the true nature and positioning of any target without the filters of programmes and expectations. This is how we punch our attention through the illusions to what is truly manifesting before us. You must do so again and again until you become an impeccable marksman because you have applied the principle so many times, to so many moving targets.

THE LIGHTS ARE ON, IS ANYONE HOME?

Listen, I do not need ten reasons why something cannot be done. I only need one reason why it can! Wandering Star

We have just explored the meditative state wherein you just witness your breath coming in and going out. This is the process that calms and stills the bodymind so we can begin to witness what really does go on inside our heads.

As you do so you become aware of all kinds of mental "chatter" and stray thoughts that are continually arising. The secret of success in meditation is to ignore them and keep witnessing the breath. This cultivates an interesting mental detachment where you can see yourself thinking and even think about what your mind is thinking about! It is proof to those who experience it that sometimes the lights are on inside our heads, there's loads of noise and chatter but no-one is home.

The negative impact in your daily life of your constant mental "noise" only becomes really apparent when you meditate. How could you ever get a clean signal from your true SELF when the lines are so busy? Besides which, these thoughts, ideas and the programmes that generate them clearly overpower your 'conscious' thinking a lot of the time, especially when you, like most people, are so often not truly present.

Remember; if you are thinking of the past or are imagining into the future, you are not here, which is where the SELF Service Universe takes down the orders. Is it really any wonder that you so often get the things and the circumstances in your life that you don't want? Those thoughts are the enemy that derail your best intentions and ruin your positive wishing by their negative thinking. Well now you can see them!

This is how you begin to see what thinking is really going on inside your head. There will be thoughts expressing as self-talk and lots of trivial bits of stuff arising. You, as the unattached observer can now start to eavesdrop on your 'mind' as it is doing its stuff.

Be sure to witness your breathing to maintain your meditative detachment and see just what it is your mind thinks about when left to its own devices. You must accept that these thoughts are using up power and are originating from your own mental equipment and thoughtscape.

Often thoughts arise that are, once seen with detachment, pretty trivial.

116

If you see this realise what a waste that is of your unlimited mental potential and resolve to not give these thoughts your attention or power. Left alone long enough through the detachment offered in meditation they can and will begin to die down. If you do find yourself caught up with a thought that's okay just stop and start again.

You begin to also witness the programmes that are the foreign installations within your operating system. You can see the attitudes, beliefs and concepts arising from your mental landscape that now are clearly from someone, somewhere else. I remember the shock of seeing programmes absorbed from my stepfather for example. I realised the voice in my head was his. How had I never known this until now?

We use meditation as the means of calming the bodymind and rendering the thoughts observable by withdrawing the normal stimuli that flood in through all our senses. In calming the bodymind we remove some of the extra power that external distractions give to our programmes and negative thinking to sneak past us and sabotage our positive wishing. We begin to see that we can still 'be' and stay aware as a functioning human without relying on what we had, up till now, thought was our mind. In truth, through identifying all the mental chatter of our ego and programmes in the meditative state we begin to master true thinking.

True thinking is a higher level of conscious and directed mental activity that has focus without loss of awareness of everything else going on in and outside our bodymind. We have gained this state when we are able to carry out all the normal routines and tasks of our daily lives and yet still have a detached mental overview of what we are doing. It is in this improved thinking level that we can spot our programmed responses and override them by will. This takes discipline to develop and perseverance. Sticking with it, being committed to mastering our own mental equipment, sees our true thinking ability improve with use. This true thinking develops our ability to concentrate fully and focus on anything that we decide requires our attention.

We also begin to cultivate what I call 'mindfulness' which is a way of being fully present in our daily lives via the observational powers of true thinking as an aspect of our real SELF. So through diligent practise of meditation in its simplest purest form we begin to develop the incredible powers of detachment and of mindfulness. By our detachment we can remove and neutralise the programmes and negative thinking and by mindfulness we are fully present to empower powerful thoughts and intentions.

That, is the real gift, the jewel of great price that meditation delivers. The powers of detachment and mindfulness exponentially increase the power you have to command the SELF Service Universe to bring forth what you truly intend. Now it is no longer a matter of wishing, it is a case of intending. You put your intent out and draw its realisation as a desired result towards you.

Your stronger and more disciplined mental activity developed through regular meditation, recognition and removal of unwanted programmes allows you to exercise free will. Negative thinking at a subconscious level can no longer influence what you want to happen. You now have the total power of your bodymind behind it as you launch your command into the SELF Service Universe fully knowing that it WILL come to pass.

Meditation also brings wellness gains too. It allows you to assist your bodymind in its duties as biological intelligence with essential tasks that do not require your conscious input or involvement. Your bodymind is amazing really. It has incredible intelligence and resources and so it can breathe, digest, repair and perform many other functions. The bodymind biological intelligence is specialised thinking capacity within your brain and specialised nerve ganglia elsewhere in the body. It is a busy little thing that records, sorts, files and manipulates all the sensory input of your wonderful vehicle of the bodymind. It monitors and controls thousands of chemical processes and regulates a range of essential body functions. Every single cell of your physical 4D vehicle, all the billions of them, is within the biological intelligence of your bodymind. It spots early warnings of trouble and defends your cells from attack by manufacturing a whole zoo of specialised cells, enzymes, proteins and essential materials. It is your loyal and untiring servant but it has been working in some terrible conditions!

You owe it to your bodymind, your biological intelligence, to give it good clean and well maintained premises and a regular supply of all the essential stores and tools for the job at hand. That is a function of wellness that we discussed earlier. So as a Spiritually Existing Love

118

Form you should have genuine love for your wonderful physical vehicle and lots of love for your dear, loyal and hardworking bodymind. So treat your vehicle lovingly and be sure to express your gratitude every now and then to your bodymind. You would be lost without it.

Meanwhile there is you, the indwelling aspect of SELF that is the owner and user of the physical vehicle. You, as an aspect of your eternal and multi-dimensional SELF are truly the dweller-in-the-machine. Meditating regularly will help you to realise this for yourself. Vipassna meditation is fantastic because it is simple and with practice it helps you realise this as an experienced truth.

I can tell you of my experience beyond the bodymind but it will be only words. The only way to know what the liberation from the bodymind is like is to experience it personally. Every meditator I have ever worked with has at some point revealed some new or different facet that appears to be uniquely their own. It would seem that, although the journey leads to the same destination, everyone's signposts and side streets are different.

By diligent practise you will soon be finding your own route and will be able to witness the breath without affecting it in any way. You, as an extension of your SELF will then be able to witness thoughts arising and passing by without being captured and distracted by them. Then one day the thoughts will stop. Yet you will still be here, witnessing the miracle of the bodymind and finally getting to know something of your true and divine nature as a being of energy manifesting into the physical realm but able to go beyond it.

Now if THAT doesn't get you interested in giving meditation a go - what will?

BUDDHA's LAST ANSWER

You might be the greatest Yak herder the world has ever seen. But you'll never know until you climb a mountain and herd some Yaks! Wandering Star

Buddha, after fulfilling over forty years of his mission, decided, as only he could, to call it a day. After all those years of serving others, of fulfilling his mission, of showing the way of enlightenment and formulating the teachings and principles that would endure for thousands of years, he was now being called by a higher power to move on. And so he sent a message to all of his disciples; "Folks, the time has come. I am to be no more. I leave you soon. Come, if you wish, before I leave."

So at the time and place his disciples gathered and he sat there peacefully, serenely, amongst this large throng from all walks of life. Princes, paupers, beggars, thieves, businessmen, former prostitutes, you name it; they were all there. There were hundreds of them. All had found something they needed and sought in Buddha and there was much wailing and lamenting because he'd said he was going. And Buddha never said anything that he didn't do. So they begged and they cajoled, they wailed and lamented as Buddha said, "For forty two years I have served you all. It comes to an end. Before I leave you, you may ask me one question, and I will answer it. So, if any of you have a question, NOW would be a good time to ask it!"

There was silence. None of the disciples wanted to be the first to ask a question. So Buddha decided it was appropriate for him to leave his bodymind and move beyond. Just as he was about to leave, a breathless figure came staggering through the crowd and fell panting heavily in front of him.

The disciples were surprised. One disciple said, "I know this man. He lives in the village thirty-odd miles away. Hey, have you run all the way?"

The man gasped, "Yes!"

The disciples were suitably astonished and asked "Why?"

"Well' replied the gasping figure, "because I heard that Buddha was dying and about to go and I wanted to ask him a question."

"Is that so?" asked the disciples "tell us then where you have come from. Where do you live?"

"I live over there!" he said pointing to the horizon from whence he'd been seen coming.

"Well Buddha has passed through your village at least thirty times that we know of in the last forty two years" they said, "so where were you? Every time he came through your village he was there for you or anyone else to come to him and ask questions. We have never seen you do this in that village. So where were you?"

"Well" he said, "one year when Lord Buddha came through the village I was so busy as my son was getting married. Oh, and another year my wife was ill. Another year, oh, I had such troubles with the cattle. Another year, Oh! Well you wouldn't believe the troubles I've had!"

And they said "But wait just a minute. For forty-two years you waited? Thirty times, at least, that this living master was in your village during that time and yet you come NOW?"

He said "Yes, But I've got a question. And Lord Buddha did say that if anyone's got a question to come and see him today and he would answer it."

At that point Buddha opened his eyes and said "He has a question for me, let him speak!"

"But master" the disciples responded "he's had forty-two years in which to talk to you and to ask any question!"

"So have you" said Buddha. "The difference is that he's waited until now to ask and you know I have to answer his question."

"This is going to be interesting" the disciples all said, "how's this guy going to ask a question, one question, after all these years, that's going to mean *anything?*"

The man was greatly relieved that he was being allowed to ask his question. So he did. Buddha listened to the question and then took him to one side and gave him the answer. And then, only then, he closed his eyes, and left.

UNDERSTANDING THIS STORY

This is a great little story. I heard a version of it several years ago from the lips of Sri Bagwan Rajneesh (later known as Osho). I cannot claim to have Bagwan as the guru that so may others did at that time, but I certainly did respect him. He was a very intelligent man with an amazing grasp of the many spiritual traditions. He also understood the power of language and was a truly hypnotic speaker. There are many books and recordings of Osho available and I include some information in the resources section at the end of this book.

So in this story the guy who arrives in the nick of time basically realised that he needed the teaching very badly. But he also knew that the teacher was no longer going to be available. He's finally realised how important the Buddha's teaching is to him, after all those years of doing absolutely nothing about it. But the source is already moving away from him and he realises that he's going to be without it very, very soon. So now, and only now, does he drop everything in his realisation of its importance and value to him.

That's a very human tendency you know. I have observed so many, many times how people seem to only truly recognise the value of something just after they realise they can't get it anymore! I have to include myself in this and be honest about not always realising what I had, right here, right now. I learned it the hard way and as this is an important point I will share that very personal lesson with you.

I came home one day a few years ago to an empty house. My wife, who had been the only partner in this life for over thirty years, had done as she'd said and left me. She had recently lost her father who was a great and wise person. We both felt his loss deeply and for thirty years he'd been my father too. She realised that she didn't want to carry on life the way it was and being an honest person she told me as gently as she could that she wanted to leave and start a fresh life. I didn't understand what she couldn't do in our life together that she could do elsewhere. But that's what she wanted and so she left. My two lovely daughters had left home before then but now, wandering through the still, empty house, my heart broke into little pieces and, for the first time in many years, I wept.

A long dormant self-pity programme saw its chance and started running in "How can I cope and carry on?" mode. You can imagine what an emotional storm I was getting myself caught up in here. She had managed our home, produced and nurtured our children and supported this crazy man in all the many and varied jobs and ventures he'd undertaken since he was sixteen. Now I was alone and I had to get to grips with the situation. I had to resist the next long-dormant but now awakening programme of the urge to fix the blame. I am grateful that I knew these programmes and could stop them quickly.

Soon enough I was back in control and started fixing the problem. It wasn't easy. I may well be a SELF-aware person with stacked deck when it comes to playing the game of life, but I still have faults and flaws. I know the power of self-pity and how real loneliness feels. Even as I know that I am never truly alone and that self-pity is a programme with no benefit whatsoever. Being smart isn't a defence against being alive in these interesting times!

Well it has been a few years now and I am getting used to living alone and most importantly I understand and am so grateful for every little and not so little thing my wife ever did for my family and me. This book is dedicated to her with that genuine gratitude.

So let me gift this great lesson to you. Without this the Law of Attraction won't work as well as it could. Take stock of your blessings and develop a genuine sense of gratitude and appreciation for everything that comes into your life. Learn to appreciate what you have. Make a point of expressing gratitude to the people and things in your life for their presence and their value to you. Do it NOW, before you have the experience of realising their value too late. This is a powerful lesson so please don't overlook it. You may feel a bit silly telling someone how grateful you are because they iron your shirts or service your car or anything else. Get over it that's just ego stuff.

Let's get back to understanding the story about Buddha and the question. A good friend of mine put it beautifully for me when he said that he had worked hard to have a sense of "havingness" in his life. How wonderful, how powerful is that?

The man in our story realised what he was about to miss and so his question to Buddha, which I didn't reveal in the story, was simply "Once you are gone how can I still get free?" What a great question! Now he clearly left it a bit late to ask it, but he was lucky. After all, he was dealing with a master, and a master of great standard. He was given the one chance he needed and he got his answer.

The answer that he was given was to become a meditator of standard and witness the illusory self, the ego, in action. Had he arrived ten minutes later it would have been a different story!

You see sometimes, no matter how careless you've been, and how much you have abused time, no matter how much you have failed to appreciate that which is there for you - which is given freely - there's still a point when you can recognise that and say "better late than never". Of course from the perspective of the methods I am putting forward in this book the better path would have been to spot the opportunity and decide "I'll do it NOW!"

For each of you seeking to realise your mission in this lifetime there is a different perception of the process. For each of you there is a different understanding of the time it will take. Just as there will be different lengths of time it has taken for you to get where you are, and to go where you need to be. But you allow so much of the things that really have nothing to do with your freedom or the well being of your SELF to get in the way.

You hang on to, and remain attached to, so many things from your past, so many programmes, fears, resentments and sorrows that don't serve the process. You make the mistake of being attached to these things, these experiences; because you feel they somehow define you. They do not. Rather than define they actually *confine* you. They are the constructs from which your ego is manufactured.

Your false self-identity relies on all this clinging and attachment for its very existence. It is this unwillingness to simply 'let go' that keeps you so securely locked into the illusions that you know you need to see through and discard. So instead be grateful and then let it all go. Dump all that past stuff and the entire ego programming into the skip of human experience and be grateful for how it didn't kill you but made you stronger and wiser. You know now that you can do it if you simply choose to. What an amazing power you have to change your life and your circumstances. Use that power and recognise how grateful you should feel for having it.

If you recognise this and commit yourselves to this process, this teaching, and act appropriately, you can still, like the man in the story, arrive breathless - but still in time! And you *know* that when you DO get around to it you will find that, as it always has been, the answer will be waiting for you.

This will take some time of course. The world you inhabit has so many ways of becoming so REAL that the true reality is hidden in the static. The 'reality' of making the mortgage payment, keeping the boss off your back and doing what you can to please others. All of it gets to be so real that the still, small voice of your SELF doesn't have much of a chance getting through. The modern world is run by the few at the expense of the many. But the many just don't seem to realise it! The controls of money, food, employment, leisure and 'spirituality' exercised by the few are extremely well tuned to keep you right where they want you to be.

There is a possibility that some of you who read this book will genuinely believe that you are pretty well off and have a 'good standard' of living. But the fuel prices, tobacco and alcohol taxes, property values, Inland Revenue dues, insurance premiums and so on are all carefully manipulated. This is done so that the majority of the law-abiding populations around the world are so wrapped up in keeping their heads financially above the water that they have no chance of waking up. You keep solvent and a decent standard of living and congratulate yourself for your 'success' as a citizen and individual. The bad things always happen to the other folks who you usually have never met and probably think you never will.

Now I know that there are more than enough 'conspiracy nuts' out there to produce the next decade's worth of X-Files episodes! But the truth is that there are forces out there that seek to keep you from realising your true nature, SELF and power. I can tell you this over and over again but as I have said before there are none as blind as the folks who won't see, and none as deaf as those won't hear.

By the way, you don't have to feel paranoid either. Paranoia is when you 'think' they are out to get you whereas knowing that they were out to get you and they've already got you isn't paranoid. It is simply becoming aware of why and how you have not yet got the life you want. Just do a bit of homework and find out for yourself just who *they* are.

The key is to just take stock of where you are. Make an honest inventory of your life and its current contents, warts and all! Appreciate all the good and enjoyable things that you have brought into your life. Express gratitude for them but also recognise all that other stuff that has come your way that you'd rather wasn't in your life. Know that the things and circumstances you now don't want came to you by infallible law from the SELF Service Universe and don't have any negative emotion or attachments about them. They simply are that's all.

Knowing what you have that you want and what you have that you don't want is important. Now you can clearly decide what else you want to bring into your life. So get a sense in the now of how so much of what you wish for and say you want hasn't yet come to pass.

In acknowledging this it is important not to indulge in any sense of lacking. If you put energy into thinking and focusing on 'not-having' then that's what you'll attract and experience courtesy of the SELF Service Universe.

So don't 'lack' anything, simply be aware of what you want but haven't yet received and then focus on a genuinely grateful sense of havingness. The power of gratitude for what we have and for what we are about to receive is a powerful vibratory force that ripples out through the SELF Service Universe and commands results.

That's important because you can attract anything you desire but haven't received once you become free from the restricting programmes and negative thinking and subconscious self-sabotage.

NOTES, IDEAS AND SCRIBBLES

This is a good place to make a list of the things and the people in your life that you are grateful for. Once you have this list you can develop that sense of 'havingness' and make an effort to express your gratitude in your daily life. It is a powerful thing that will bring more positivity into your life!

THE SCULPTOR

All things in the world are two. In our minds we are two – good and evil. With our eyes we see two things – things that are fair and things that are ugly. We have the right hand that strikes and makes for evil, and the left hand full of kindness, near the heart. One foot may lead us to an evil way, the other foot may lead us to a good. So are all things two, all two.
Eagle Chief (Letakoks-Lesa) Pawnee.

One day a long time ago there lived a wise old master sculptor of great skill and fame. It was said that when he sculpted a bird you could almost hear the feathers rustling. His art was the finest and his fame was well deserved. In this story we join the master sculptor one day as he was working in his studio. He was busily working on a beautiful new statue and one of his new apprentices was standing nearby watching his every move intently. This apprentice was determined not to miss the slightest thing because, one day, he too wanted to be a master sculptor with a studio of his own! He had spent all his time watching his master and he was constantly in awe of him. Other apprentices in the studio were less dedicated and less ambitious and often made fun of him for being so quiet and so shy of the master.

Finally, the apprentice managed to overcome his shyness and gather up enough courage to approach the great artist. "Master, may I ask you a question?" he asked timidly.

"Of course you may" replied the master gently "for asking a question is one of many paths to knowledge and wisdom. Please, ask of me what you will." The master was smiling and encouraging the apprentice. He had already sensed that this youngster was unlike the other apprentices and would be the only one invited to stay and study the art.

"Well" the apprentice began nervously, "I can see that you are creating yet another beautiful statue. But it started out, only a short while ago, as nothing more than a large, crude block of marble. Just like this one here." He pointed to the large roughly hewn block of stone in front of him. It was bigger than he was!

"True" replied the sculptor "but what is the question?"

"What I would like to know is how you actually DO it! For example, can you please tell me how you could carve an elephant out of this block of stone?"

The sculptor smiled. He was a kindly man and had been waiting patiently for this young man to ask exactly such a question. "Well" he explained gently "I take the chisel in my left hand like this. Then I take my mallet in my right hand and hold it like this. Then I place the chisel against the stone block, strike it with the chisel and simply chip away everything that doesn't look like an elephant!"

WHAT IS THIS ABOUT?

Now the process that I, as one of the vehicles for this teaching, have undertaken with each of the students seeking to become free, is very much like the master sculptor's method of sculpting an elephant! Through this book I am guiding you to help you see the simple truth. I am guiding you towards understanding that the means for becoming free, for accessing your true SELF is very much like the master sculptor's method for sculpting that elephant.

You are an energy field that has a body, not a body that has an energy field. This means that you are a superb sculpture that has become a rough block by what has been added to you. The process of becoming free and accessing your SELF is the chipping away and removal of all that is not who and what *you* truly are. We know that the detachment of meditation and mindfulness in our daily lives are the keys to this.

It is this process of recognising and undoing the programmes and negative habits that eventually reveals the true aspect of the eternal SELF dwelling within those who undertake this journey. The bits we chip away are the programmes and the thought habits that we have, through meditation and mindfulness, identified as 'foreign installations' and therefore have no place in the life of any being who desires to be free.

The chisel, mallet and the vision of what is within are my gifts to you through this teaching and this process. The mallet represents the force of your will to keep chipping away for as long as it takes. This takes commitment and as we now know, that means something quite specific. You must keep going not just as long as is convenient but for as long as it takes. This takes you outside of your comfort zone. If it is uncomfortable it is to be celebrated because, for a rare moment, you have committed beyond your normally limiting comfort zone which is, in iteslf, powered and sustained by a whole bunch of programmes.

The chisel represents the ability to precisely target the programmes, negative habits and illusions that have attached themselves to your true being. You do this through the detachment from your bodymind and mental chatter you achieve in meditation. This allows you to truly see the things arising, the thoughts and programmes that are clearly not you at all. They are moving targets but at least they have become illuminated in the spotlight and can be recognised again and again.

The vision of the master sculptor is the ability to see inside the block and recognise the sculpture that already exists. In so doing he can help the dweller within to see this too. The role is to see and point out the truth of who and what you have become. I can do this from where I stand and help you to step outside, however briefly, to see it too. This is not an easy task for either of us. Whoever you find as your mentor and guide on this path must have that vision, that 'seeing' too. The seeing is the key that empowers you until you can see too. By diligent practise of meditation and mindfulness you gain the insight - the seeing within - that is necessary in identifying what the teacher already sees.

Whereas the pupil only saw a large block of stone, the master sculptor obviously saw much, much more. Clearly from where he stood it wasn't like that at all. One block was, through his skill, already realising its potential as a beautiful statue. The other block selected by the apprentice was just waiting. It was pregnant with all the possible statues that the master could see within it. All that was required was for him to remove that which was not the thing he saw inside. Then the potential would become reality!

And that is what you must do too if you want to become free. You need to identify all that is not the true you that is the aspect of your eternal SELF and begin to chip away at it. Soon you will get a part of the true you cleared and the task will become easier. Starting out from the beginning and seeing all the artificial you that you thought was real is understandably not the nicest thing to experience. But you have a distinct advantage in that, unlike the statues, you are not something imaginary projected within. You, each and every one of you, already *are* beautiful works of art. The beauty and power of the real you planted within by your SELF isn't the illusion, the block is.

If I am with you then I look at you and see the kind of shape you're in. What I and others like me are seeing is that which has been added both with and without your knowledge and consent. We see the illusions that you have accepted as real. As long as you cannot see beyond the illusions and programmes you are blocking yourself off from your true being. You cannot begin to fully access the power of the SELF Service Universe to change your life and circumstances. The art is to see through all of that stuff that has been added to you from the moment that you became a part of this crazy 4D universe.

You, the real aspect of your eternal SELF (Spiritually Existing Love Form) that is the many manifesting as one in order to dance with the possibilities of this vehicle, cannot be hidden from me or the other masters out there. The master's task, and the purpose of this teaching, is to reach in to awaken you from your sleep and dreaming. To pierce the veil of illusion to remind you of your truth and beauty as a compassionate being of light in the spiritual dimensions that came into your current bodymind vehicle to experience, develop, serve and grow. Whether you currently remember this simple truth or not, that's exactly why you came here.

But on your journey life, your parents, your experiences, your wants, desires and all of that stuff have slapped bits onto you. They have encased and trapped you in a heavy coat of illusion and programmes. These programmes and illusions have deceived you, stolen our freedom, put the true you to sleep and weighted you down. A programme or two were plastered onto you there. A couple of false expectations have been slapped on real thick up here. A desire or two have been slapped on down there. All of these additions are concealing and blocking off the being within.

They are also stifling the warmth and compassion that you have to offer to other sentient beings here in the 4D. So slowly you have been built up into blocks of ego and programmes set in stone. You become blocks that are convinced that they are the statues, the work of art. Having been so fooled by the illusion and programming you carry on deceiving yourself and continue the process of enlarging that casing, that restriction on being. This way you are literally blocking your SELF off from your true potentials so you end up alongside so much of humanity as just so many blocks that cannot move freely and express the truth imprisoned within, but still thinking they are okay and have free will.

131

The good news is that the whole thing is totally reversible. That which has been added to you that is false and does not serve you can be chipped away. You can work through the programmes and ego to reveal and realise the true you and access your SELF. You can shed all that negative and inappropriate stuff and reconnect with your SELF. That is how you become free and allow your life to manifest to its full potential within this 4D space-time universe. You can make a difference and claim the power that is yours. The SELF Service Universe awaits your orders.

THE BREATH IS THE LIFE
Life without limitations is about spreading your wings and taking flight. You don't know which direction to go? Never mind, you flap and I'll steer! Wandering Star

As we have already seen, meditation is the simplest and most powerful tool for stilling the bodymind so we can see what blocks our true power. It gives us the power, like the master sculptor in the last story, to see the true beauty within. So we use meditation as the simple tool for stilling the bodymind. To be more specific, we still the bodymind through the simple meditative act of witnessing our breathing. Now that is, as we know, easier said than done.

The moment you pay attention to your breathing you interrupt its normally automatic nature. Just by observing your breathing you somehow signal the bodymind control centre that says "Oh hi there! You want to take over? Okay well control is yours." This is something that most people experience when starting to meditate. The problem is that breathing is normally an automated event that we pay little attention to. The moment we are asked to observe our breathing we find that our attention interferes and stops it from being automatic. So then we end up having to 'do' the breathing and now our focus is on doing rather than simply witnessing.

That is a problem because if you are paying attention and effort in doing something you are not meditating. However if you can let go of any attachment to taking control of the breathing your body will once again resume the automatic actions. Your body has been doing this since you came into this crazy 4D realm so you'd hope that you would know how to do it properly. Surprisingly, that's not quite how it turns out because we do often interrupt the autonomous breathing and instil some bad habits when we do. To fully explain this I need to just take one of my small diversions.

I have a good friend who is a true Shaman and an amazing healer. I am grateful that she's around to help me from time to time. You see I'm just as likely as anyone else to end up tense and burdened with negative energy that I have picked up in my work. When you work with many people who are attempting to become free you often take on some of their "stuff" as part of the process.

Some healers will be of service to others by absorbing and carrying away negative energies when it is appropriate to do so. I often use this technique when the patient's energy systems are badly depleted or out of balance. At such times I might be able to discharge the negative energies and associated physical effects by uplinking to my SELF, or I might, on occasion need some help. When I need that kind of help my friend gives freely of her skills in this area.

When she gets her hands on me she will detect and then chase any knots and energy blocks around my body (yes they move the little devils!) until she finally gets them out. Now it can sometimes be quite painful. She is a very small person but the strength of those hands when they detect a knot or block is quite awesome! At such times she can often be heard saying to me "you must breathe! Come on breathe it out!" She knows the importance of breathing. More importantly we both know the importance of breathing properly as the situation or circumstances demands.

You would be surprised to learn that both my friend and I come across very few people who actually breathe properly! Even when it is on the automatic system the breathing isn't as nature intended. Now breathing is kind of basic don't you think? If you don't eat you can last a considerable time. If you don't drink water you can still last for days. However, if you don't breathe you won't last more than a few minutes, so I guess that tells us how vital the breath is.

So if breathing is that basic to our survival how can people not be doing it correctly? How is it possible for people to not know how to breathe the way their bodymind requires them to do so for optimum health and longevity? This is so important a subject that it's getting this whole (and longer than usual) chapter devoted to it. I could actually write several on this one subject and have come across entire books written many years ago by various people on the simple matter of breathing.

The breath is the life. More importantly breathing is the mechanism by which the energy of life is absorbed and sent around the body revitalising and detoxifying every single cell in it. Now some of you will have already assumed I am talking about Oxygen and Carbon Dioxide. That is the main physical aspect of the breathing process at a physical level but there is certainly more to it than this.

Breathing also brings into the body the subtle energy known to the ancients as 'Prana', which translates as 'absolute energy'. This energy is what powers the subtle energy circuitry of the bodymind and it has its source in the universal field at the quantum level. In its positive and life enhancing form (light wavelengths and frequencies) I call the Pranic energy packets 'Lifetrons'. When, as happens through the electromagnetic fog we discussed earlier, the energy is in negative and damaging wavelengths and frequencies I call the energy packets 'Deathtrons'. I do this because it is helpful for the student in visualising and understanding their existence and effects when necessary.

It doesn't take a genius to work out that we need to secure ample supplies of Lifetrons whilst expelling and avoiding any build up of Deathtrons. Because we are exposed to these energies mainly through the air we breathe (they're present also in energy fields around us) you can see the importance of understanding the science of breath. Breathing properly enhances life and improper breathing doesn't. However I know that Deathtrons can also enter and penetrate the skin of the body through exposure to strong electromagnetic fields that comprise the man-made electromagnetic fog surrounding and penetrating the planet today.

So it is reassuring and vital to know that proper breathing as a habit can so charge and maintain the body's Lifetronic field that it effectively becomes a shield that deflects large numbers of Deathtrons every millisecond.

So what does proper breathing mean? Everyone you meet who is currently alive in this 4D universe must be breathing. So if they are not breathing properly what are they doing?

Firstly, proper breathing is that by which the full available capacity of the lungs is utilised and the rate of breathing in, holding and breathing back out optimises the transfer of oxygen to the cells and the efficient elimination of toxins. It can also, in recognition of the subtle Pranic nature of air, be characterised as building and maintaining a healthy accumulation of Lifetrons whilst eliminating and guarding against Deathtrons.

Secondly, improper breathing is the manifestation of bad habits, incorrect usage of the diaphragm and other muscles, and a result of poor posture.

Once you understand the physical aspects of proper breathing you can observe people around you and you will probably find that there are three main types of improper breathing. These can be described as:

(1) High Breathing

(2) Mid Breathing

(3) Low Breathing

Let me just give you a very quick idea of these three types of breathing and then we'll move on to the correct method.

The first incorrect breathing pattern is called "high breathing" and it is a very common occurrence. I have heard it referred to, in yogic circles, as a phenomenon more common in western peoples. I see it all around me (especially in smokers) and hope some of those people come across something like this book! As the name describes the breathing all takes place in the upper chest and collarbone region and so the smallest part of the lungs is being used. This means that no more than half the full lung capacity is being used. It is an energy intensive method of breathing for the body with little payoff! A lot of high breathers also tend to breathe through an open mouth most of the time thus bypassing all the wonderful design and usefulness of the nasal filters etc.

The second method of respiration I called "mid breathing" and again the name gives a definite clue as to what is going on. The diaphragm pushes upwards, the ribs are raised and the mid region of the chest area expands slightly. Again the full useful capacity of the lungs, as provided by nature as a vital mechanism of life, is not being utilised and some parts of the lower lungs and upper areas rarely get purged with fresh air.

The third is called the "low breathing"; method and I guess by now you've got the hang of this and know what I am about to say! Yes, this is what we would call abdominal or diaphragm breathing. It is far better than the two preceding methods as it certainly allows a "deeper" breath and aerates much more of the lung capacity. So if you are going to take conscious control to improve the quality of your breathing and gain health benefits this low breathing method is where you need to start.

If you are not quite familiar with the diaphragm then you should be as we all have one! It is a great slab of muscle, which separates the chest and its contents from the abdomen and its contents. If you were inside your abdomen looking up at your diaphragm it would be like an arched ceiling and viewed from the chest it would be a dome-like hill. This muscle is the key to breathing in us humans (and other mammals) and we can gain conscious control of it.

So to sum up so far; high breathing only fills the upper lung area, mid breathing fills only the mid-lung region and a part of the upper area, and low breathing fills the lower and middle regions but gets the most air into your lungs of the three.

So what is the correct or most beneficial way to breathe? That would be what we shall call the "complete breath' and this method removes all the negatives of the other methods by bringing into action all the available lung capacity and utilises all the muscles associated with expanding the chest, ribs and diaphragm. As you become accustomed to breathing completely you also tone all the associated muscles, provide internal massage to many vital organs, increase oxygenation and de-toxification of blood and tissues. You also will find that your chest and lung capacity will increase as the ribs achieve their maximum range of expansion.

So I think we can safely say that if the breath is the life and the source of the most fundamental vitality for the human system, it would be a pretty good idea to learn more about getting the most of it through mastering our breathing. There are many benefits to be had from learning to breathe the way nature intended so let us now take the time to study and acquire the complete breath for ourselves.

The complete breath is the correct method of breathing, which has been known to practitioners of Yogic Science for millennia. However, the average person who doesn't happen to be a Yogi or attend training in the science needs to know this method and to use it.

That means explaining it here without any jargon or mysticism so that all us non-yogis can get on with our lives with the added advantage of breathing the way nature intended and in the way that is absolutely best for us. Fair enough, as part of my ongoing mission I am happy to oblige so read on.

THE COMPLETE BREATH

To shine brightly so that others may see. To give your heart so that others may love. To serve so that others may become free: that is the glory burning bright within you. Wandering Star

Having already explained how most people develop one of three common poor breathing habits we now need to look at a solution. The low, mid and high breathing habits have varying degrees of negative effects on the bodymind. It is clearly better, having explored the power of the breath and the apparatus nature has supplied, to develop correct breathing. The best way to teach you the Complete Breath is to provide you with some simple and easy to follow instructions. You should read through this section first to make sure you understand it and can visualise the movements that are involved. Then you should find somewhere quiet where you will be undisturbed for a while and actually carry out the instructions, referring to these pages as you do so.

Before we begin I want to just emphasise that the Complete Breath is not a forced or unnatural thing. In fact it is the opposite as it takes us back to how nature intended us to breathe. The tiny infant of today naturally uses the Complete Breath, as did our savage ancestors who lived and survived in the wild. But the average civilised modern human has clearly forgotten how to breathe this way and has thus lost a fundamental part of keeping the physical vehicle in good condition. It amazes me how people who own cars will spend money to ensure their motor has a clean air filter fitted. They do this so the engine can breathe properly and yet they fail to ensure the same service for their own body! I will be a good boy and avoid pouring too much scorn on those folks who also smoke and deliberately pollute their lungs.

If you have stayed with me this far you will realise that your personal wellness has much to gain from making the most of your lungs. We have already mentioned that air contains more than just oxygen and the trace gases necessary for biological respiration. The Pranic energy, the Lifetrons, deliver vitality to the subtler energy components of our bodymind. Even putting aside the finer aspects the simple act of utilising all the lung area and all the associated muscles has clear and measurable physical benefits. Regularly sweeping all the airways with warm fresh air ensures that pockets of stagnant air do not have a chance to build up. We also already know the increased oxygenation and removal of carbon dioxide is beneficial to the whole organism.

I also want to advise you that the Complete Breath doesn't call for the complete filling of every part of the lungs with every inhalation. In other words Complete Breathing doesn't need to be continuous deep breathing. You can inhale an average amount of air using the Complete Breath to distribute it to all parts of the lungs. However, for real benefits you should deliberately make several full capacity Complete Breaths several times a day.

The following simple exercise will help you to begin mastering the Complete Breath:

Stand or sit erect. If you are seated rest your hands lightly along the tops of your thighs. If you are standing, have your feet slightly apart and let your arms hang loosely at your sides. Keep your neck straight, your chin up slightly and look straight ahead of you. This ensures that your airways are relaxed and fully open.

Breathing in through the nose begin to inhale steadily and evenly, first filling the lower part of the lungs by consciously pushing downwards with your diaphragm. This downward and outward expansion puts a gentle massaging pressure on the abdominal organs and you can feel your lower belly swelling out. Continue the inhalation and now fill the middle part of your lungs by expanding your ribcage. Finally, as the inward breath continues, you can fill the top of your lungs by deliberately lifting and expanding your upper chest. This final stage will automatically pull the lower abdomen back inwards slightly to support the lungs.

Once the lungs are full and you cannot expand your ribcage and chest any more you stop inhaling and pause for a few seconds just holding all that air in your fully filled lungs.

Now begin to exhale through your slightly open mouth. You need to expel all the air in one long, smooth, slow outward breath. The way to do this is to push slowly upwards with your diaphragm. As the air leaves you will naturally feel your ribcage begin to move back and your chest will also relax and contract. Once all the air is out of your lungs, close your mouth, pause for a few seconds and then begin once again to inhale through your nose. That is one Complete Breath.

There you have it. At first I am sure you will be concentrating on each of the three distinct movements of diaphragm, ribs and chest as you inhale. This can make the inward breath cycle jerky if you are not careful. So with this in mind persevere and aim to achieve the union of all three motions into one uniform continuous inhalation. However, in a very short time if you practise you'll very quickly become familiar and comfortable with the technique. Then your inward breath will become one long smooth action that incorporates the three stages. Then your outward exhalation, after the pause, will also become a continuous flow from expansion to relaxation of the involved body parts.

Please practise this Complete Breath and be sure to give every bit of it your fullest attention. Be totally present as you carry out the Complete Breath. It will bring you very real benefits and hopefully it will develop to become a valuable and lifelong habit.

I hope that you will also pass the technique on to others who you observe to be breathing incorrectly. Everyone stands to gain a great deal from breathing the way nature intended. I promise no cures or miracles but as a lifelong Complete Breather I have a massive chest expansion, very rarely ever get colds, flu or coughs and, as an opera singer I can't half hold a note for long time!

Correct breathing is an essential part of bodymind maintenance and also leads to an improvement in one's speaking voice and increased vitality. I heartily recommend it to you knowing that your heart will be most grateful if you master the Complete Breath.

NOTES, IDEAS AND SCRIBBLES

YOU'LL SEE IT WHEN YOU BELIEVE IT!

I cannot believe that the purpose of life is to simply be happy. I think that the purpose of life is to be useful, to be responsible, to be compassionate. It is, above all, to matter: to count and stand for something, to have made some difference that you have lived at all. Leo C Rosten

The process being described in this book is designed to set you free. It cannot be said too many times that you are an energy field that has a body, not a body that has an energy field. That energy field has been described to you as the SELF, the Spiritually Existing Love Form that has its residence within the multi-dimensional quantum field that permeates this and all possible universes. This field, this SELF can also be called the Soul but in our understanding this soul is beyond any religious definitions that impose any characteristics or limitations upon it. So if it helps you can say that you are a soul with a body, not a body with a soul.

The idea that you can, through the process described in this book, reconnect with your SELF, your soul and then become free to live the life you want is incredibly powerful and liberating. That's if you are able to overcome some of the limiting thought habits and negative programmes long enough to recognise the truth of it. The problem that often arises in this process is one of belief. I have a specific view of belief and I would like to explore it with you.

I often hear people when they are confronted with something that challenges their negative thinking and expectations declaring that they'll believe it *when* they see it. I have to say that under many such situations it is not surprising when they don't see it and enjoy telling me that they'd told me so! They have totally missed the point. They needed to realise that when they believed it *then* they would see it. Do you see the difference?

Believing positively can be a powerful tool for overcoming the negative thoughts that hide inside our minds. The negative thoughts that are programmed into us can, and do, usually sabotage any positive wishing we might indulge in. As we have grown up we have accepted limiting beliefs that were someone else's opinion of our ability or more to the point, our supposed lack of ability.

The child who is overweight and is bullied and taunted as slow and dim will, eventually, re-programme their self-image accordingly. They not only think they are fat and inferior, they also believe it. As an adult they will still be overweight and will limit themselves in their personal and professional lives to maintain the image that was programmed. Even if they diet and study they will often fail to lose the weight or advance academically because their wishes and actions are in direct conflict with their thoughts and belief. Victims who were programmed to accept their fate tend to stay victims and aggressors who have been programmed to use force to get ahead tend to continue to be aggressive. Their beliefs are as negative as their thought habits and this is a double whammy that will ensure that what they believe they will see.

So what is my view, my personal understanding of belief? To my way of seeing things, belief appears to be a convenient mental conditioning that allows someone to accept something as true and real without any attempt to actually verify it. Even if there is evidence to contradict their belief it will not persuade them to change the mental conditioning. This mental conditioning is so powerful that it can ignore any sensory input that contradicts it.

That's not so terrible if the belief in question is positive in nature and has beneficial effect. But a great majority of beliefs seem to be of the negative variety that limit and restrict people's potential and reduce their self-worth. The SELF Service Universe is totally and utterly impartial when it comes to taking its orders and manifesting things and circumstances. Negative beliefs routinely deliver negative results even if their owner had been wishing positively.

The dilemma here is that belief actually accesses the same energies and power of thought that conscious intent uses to invoke the universal law of attraction. As I have just said, this law is totally impersonal and manifests whatever the mental energy has imagined. So if most beliefs are actually negative in effect, programmed into the human hard drive by external authorities as a means of control and containment then we know what the results are going to be. Very few so called 'personal' beliefs that people cling to, when analysed and traced back through the chain of cause and effect, can be seen to have originated within them or been accepted through free will. So the many beliefs that have been programmed into us are more likely to be in the best interests of someone, or something else. They will not serve our efforts to become free and reconnected to our SELF and our power to control our own lives.

We have already looked at the simple fact that most of us don't get what we want out of life. More often than not we actually end up on the receiving end of the things we don't want. We do so because although we wish positively, our programmes, beliefs and experiences ensure that, usually below our conscious awareness, we think negatively. This is important. We need to be clear that a great deal of the time this negative thinking is happening at a level below our immediate awareness. So we have to develop strategies for becoming aware of these hidden thoughts and negative mental energies. We are seeking to ensure we have conscious control of our bodymind so we can wish positively and think positively. You see our thoughts are incredibly powerful and they can easily overpower any wishes we make.

Thoughts become things. Please understand that it really is that simple. This is a very important and powerful lesson so please read it as many times as it takes for you to feel you understand it. I'll say it again, <u>thoughts make things</u>. Everything that you see around you that is manufactured in any way must have started out as a thought. Whatever is existing that is not a naturally occurring creation of nature could not, and did not, suddenly just pop into existence. The mobile phone, for example, didn't just appear on someone's desk and everyone who saw it went "ooh, look at that! Let's call it a mobile phone." No the mobile phone came from the telephone and the radio which came from experiments and thoughts of such people as Marconi and Bell.

There's a chain of cause and effect, the results of interdependent reality, that accounts for these things but their source is human thought. The house you live in, the clothes you wear, the car you drive all began as human thoughts sometime, somewhere. The reason these things exist in the 4D is because the thoughts that are their primary cause were not opposed and overpowered and so the effect of their becoming objects was created. The instructions sent to the SELF Service Universe got there and were acted upon. Once the SSU has got the order it will deliver exactly to specification.

Thoughts can and do become things, whether they are good or bad. Many thoughts will create things that do not add to the quality of human lives or improve the environment. But if not opposed or overpowered by other factors these things thought of will be acted upon by the SSU and they'll manifest sooner or later. This is a simple law backed up by interdependent reality. It is cause and effect as discussed earlier in this book.

What is equally important and relevant to you in creating the life that you desire, is that thoughts also direct human actions and inaction. As a person thinks so will they be. The dominant thoughts whether they are conscious or subconscious will make the man. Or at the very least they make the circumstances that surround him. In this manner thoughts, when they are not becoming things, are becoming circumstances instead. You need to understand just how powerful your thoughts are, especially the hidden ones below your conscious awareness. They are powerful at this time because they are creating the circumstances of your life. A lot of your moment by moment actions, inaction and responses to the world around you are being governed by your subconscious thinking.

If you gain better control of your bodymind and recognise these subconscious thoughts and programmes, you can then generate conscious thoughts to disable them. Then through directed conscious thought you will generate things through the SELF Service Universe and create circumstances more in tune with your desires. Of course all things are connected and so you also have to recognise that the power of other people's thoughts, especially those controlled by their beliefs, can and do impact upon you.

As the thoughts of others occur around you they have an effect on how your circumstances develop unless they are opposed and overpowered. So it is a very good idea to surround yourself with good people. Be sure to spend time with others who are supportive of your dreams or at the very least do not dismiss them. This is vital so please don't miss it.

You need to be sure that the people you are spending time with are not messing with your orders to the SSU. We all know people who seem to enjoy shooting us down at every opportunity. They like to argue and take the opposite of whatever we say or do. Such people are not in harmony with you or the life you want. You should keep your distance form people like this and follow your dreams with people who are on the same wavelength as you. A group of friends and like-minded people united with a shared dream or goal is an incredibly powerful device for giving 'express delivery' orders to the SELF Service Universe!

So if we must have belief, if we need for some reason to accept as true something that we have no proof for, then let us at least make our belief serve us and those we care to share our dreams with. Let's have positive life affirming belief that undoes the effects of subconscious and conscious negative thinking. A strong belief can, as we have already seen, oppose and overpower a wish or thought.

The power of a consciously directed positive thought or belief appears to be several times more powerful than a negative subconscious one. So a positive belief can make short work of any negativity and that has to be an improvement. You can have beliefs that use the law that thoughts make things to get better circumstances into your life. In such cases I can tell you that you won't believe it when you see it, you'll see it when you believe it.

At this point it would be very useful for you to just pause and consider what sort of beliefs you do have. You probably have never actually sat down before to locate and list your beliefs. They are not too hard to find once you start looking for them. They shape the way you think, the way you feel, and the way react to events and circumstances in your life. So in a real sense a lot of your actions and reactions in life are directly manipulated to keep you in line with your beliefs. Let's be clear about this, belief is incredibly powerful and, if it is in the negative, it can really screw up your life and derail even your best intentions.

So if you are going to have beliefs then it is a very good idea to check them and, where necessary, adjust them from a negative viewpoint to a positive one. That sounds simpler than it actually is because you may not have had much experience yet of doing a one-eighty. You might remember that earlier in this book I mentioned that it's a good idea to begin looking at things from the other way round? I said that a situation that viewed from one way appears to be a problem, can when viewed from turning it one hundred and eighty degrees, actually become an opportunity.

That is the key. You see the potential for hidden negative beliefs to impact on your conscious positive wishing will always be there. That means that the SELF Service Universe will act impartially upon the order it receives even if it isn't what you think you have asked for. So by getting to know what you DO believe and then doing some work on ensuring they are all positive in effect is a great thing. Then you can start to look forward to getting what you want rather than what your old negative beliefs used to order instead. That is a worthwhile activity isn't it?

Here are a few examples of negative beliefs that people have:
- There are always problems in my life.
- I'm never going to be good enough.
- Once bitten, twice shy so I must avoid getting hurt.
- If it hasn't happened yet I guess it never will.
- Better not wish for too much I'll only get hurt.
- I should have worked this out by now.
- Nobody will like me because I'm different.
- I need more money to pay my bills.
- One day I'll get what I want.

So let's look at these negative, limiting beliefs and do a few one-eighties. We can restate our negative and limiting beliefs in a positive and unlimiting way. So in order from the first list these beliefs can become something like this:
- Every problem is an opportunity in disguise.
- I am always improving and getting better.
- What doesn't kill me makes me stronger.
- It doesn't matter when it happens I know it will.
- I don't mind getting hurt in order to get what I want.
- I learn by doing.
- I am unique and that makes me interesting to others.
- I attract money frequently and easily.
- Every day takes me nearer my goals.

I hope you will take the time to just review what I did here and have a go for yourself. Take a few moments to examine your own beliefs. Ask yourself honestly what you believe in. Take a few moments and write some of them down here. This is a useful exercise that sounds easy but I think you'll find getting to grips with what you truly believe might take some work. There's no hurry so take your time. Don't forget there's every possibility that you have beliefs that have been sabotaging your positive wishing for years. What do you have to lose? Go on, list them here:

_____

_____

_____

_____

_____

_____

_____

If you have written down something then you have done well and it shows that you are committed to making the circumstances in your life change by changing yourself and your thinking. Now why not have some fun, with a useful purpose, and have a go at re-writing those beliefs in the most positive way you can. If you find it difficult you can remember the old one-eighty trick. For example "I am anti-war" sounds okay; no-one is going to argue that that's not a well intentioned belief. But the signal it sends the SELF Service Universe and draws through the Law of Attraction is about war and must be negative in vibration. The same belief in the positive is "I am pro-peace". Do you see the difference? You are not changing what you believe and care strongly about; you are simply giving it a positive vibration and thus empowering it to attract positive results. So see if you can work some one-eighty magic on your beliefs. Have a go now.

_____

_____

_____

_____

_____

_____

_____

So after all I have said about believing, do I believe in anything? The answer is a simple "no" and I will explain why. You see I discovered the mainly illusory and often negative aspects of human belief a long time ago. I observed the incredible power of belief to deny any truth and contradictory evidence and decided I didn't want to limit my free SELF in that way. I know that the power of knowing far exceeds the power of belief.

Knowing requires no faith that might waver and requires no hope that might turn out to be unfulfilled. When I know something to be so then it has the full power of total conviction with no niggling doubts to bleed away its power. No I don't believe anything at all. What I do is to operate and manifest in the 4D realm by means of a threefold system. To me there are three states that apply to everything within the 4D universe:

- I know something IS
- I know something IS NOT
- I know that something IS YET TO RESOLVED

The conviction, the lack of doubt that is the characteristic of true knowing makes it possible to focus tremendous power on one's mental processes. It takes an awful lot of negative energy to overpower true knowledge.

I understand that I am I a rare and fortunate position with this knowing I have. That comes mainly from my unusual mental capabilities, vast experience and a lot of regular help from my true SELF. As you move through life you will explore and experience many things and gain knowledge that will no longer need you to believe. Don't worry for now

149

belief is good as long as it is positive and not limiting your ability to attract what you want from the universe. For now it is simply that you believe and I know.

By the way I am incredibly grateful to have developed this mental approach at an early age. The power of conviction has allowed me to experience so many different situations and circumstances in my life. As stated in the introduction to this book my curriculum vitae looks like I should be at least a couple of hundred years older than I am to have done so many things! My knowing has also enabled me to work effectively with people on their mission to become free. In the face of my knowing their programmes, negative thinking and limiting beliefs usually don't survive too long. The removal of those aspects of their ego and programming that do not serve gives them a useful boost on the journey to freedom.

I am also excited and grateful for this experience of manifesting in the 4D universe. It is so vast and full of wonders that it has given me so many things that are yet to be resolved. The adventure of finding out eventually which way such things will turn out (is, or is not) gives me tremendous fun and pleasure.

:

WHAT DO YOU WANT?

Even though you have 10,000 fields, you can only eat one measure of rice a day; even though your dwelling contains 1,000 rooms you can only use eight feet of space at night.
Chinese Saying.

We are nearly at our destination. We have certainly come a long way together. We have explored nearly all the key factors that put our personal power, wishing, thinking and intent together. We need to combine them into a focussed laser-like command to the unlimited resources of the SELF Service Universe. When we are able to do that life is going to become an incredible, exciting adventure as we reach for the top. So now is NOT the time to quit when you are closer to the destination than the start. No, you are really closing in on your best most desired life and there are just a couple of things I need to share with you.

As we know, the biggest and most difficult challenge facing all of us in this crazy 4D realm is to understand our own responsibility for what comes into, or out of, our lives. We are, indeed, the architects of our own fortune, or misfortune, and we can live our whole lives without ever knowing we'd drawn up the plans! It is astonishing that so many lives are designed and then built without the architect ever visiting the building site to see what is being done with the design. It is that lack of presence, the being here in the now, that allows the programmes to basically mess up what was supposed to be a dream dwelling. If you are not present when the construction of your life is taking place, you are not really in much of a position to complain that it isn't what you wanted.

That lack of presence and understanding of our personal power as architect of our lives is why so many people continue to get what they don't want, and don't get what they do want. That is a great pity and also a massive loss of human potential for individuals and the world. That is why I wrote this book and why you have been reading it to get this far. So that you can see that beyond your positive wishing or cosmic ordering are the sabotaging beliefs and negative thinking arising from your programmes. This thinking, even if it is mostly unconscious or not normally within your attention, is what is powering the events and outcomes of your life.

151

Thoughts, as we know, become things. Even if those things have been ordered by your submerged fears and negativity. Whatever is the subject of our most dominant thoughts will eventually manifest in our lives. Someone once said that 'as a man thinks today, so does he become tomorrow'. So our dominant or most common thoughts are very relevant to how our life is unfolding. You place your order with every thought and, when enough signal strength has been established, the order gets received, processed by the SELF Service Universe and shipped accordingly.

But the real challenge facing us on this journey towards getting free and securing a better, happier and wealthier life is also incredibly simple. It is to get to grips with our wanting. Desire is a powerful force in our lives. There is nothing wrong about wanting. The problem is that very few people know what they really want. You might have missed that so let's hit the replay button: very few people know what they really want.

Now you might be tempted to say that I have made a mistake here. After all I have referred all the way through this book to people positively wishing but negatively thinking and getting what they don't want rather that what they do want. But think about it for a moment and do a one-eighty on this. Most people are very capable of endorsing what I have said because what they really know is what they don't want. That is absolutely clear because that's what most of them are fed up of getting! As you are reading this book I can safely include you as one who would like to change this habit.

Please consider this: The SELF Service Universe is infallible. By law it will respond to your dominant thoughts and bring to you what you think about most. So if you keep getting stuff that you say you don't want you clearly score maximum points for being one who knows what they don't want. It's just that you and many others fail to do the one-eighty and recognise that the other point of view indicates that you and they do not know what is really wanted.

Now I am sure that once people begin to be exposed to this teaching and the methods that many self-help mentors and I are putting forward things will change. I cannot and will not condemn you for failing to act upon the simple one-eighty technique because you probably never knew about it. The good news is that you do now and it is a simple and powerful technique that you can decide to use.

So right here and now ask yourself this very short and simple question; <u>what do I want?</u>

If you can answer this question and say that what you want is your dominant thought until it is realised then you are very unusual and are probably another self-help mentor just checking my book out! Anyway the question stands; what do you want?

Please give yourself a minute and stop here, now and give this question your full attention. Almost immediately you will have mentally answered the question with other questions. They probably have to do with whether the question takes into consideration other factors or limits such as money, time etc. If you think that isn't the case that's fine but be certain that you haven't overlooked the thoughts and beliefs operating below your conscious threshold. We have already begun to use techniques to reveal their existence and to eventually identify their contents.

But let's keep pressing ahead with this subject of what you want. You need to be able to state what you want as a goal as something that you can work towards in partnership with the SSU. For our purposes we don't want to aim low at this point. You need to come up with something so really big and exciting that the realisation of it will change your life forever. Please think about this. If you aim for the stars and fall short you can still end up on the moon. But if you aim for the moon and fall short you are still here on the ground. So what you decide you want right now needs to be inspired and ambitious enough to really stretch you.

We spend an awful lot of time in our heads caught up in our thoughts and programmes. It is important to remember we have a heart too. There is real benefit to be had from moving from thinking to feeling when appropriate. A goal that is worthy of us should appeal both to our head and our heart and so motivate and inspire us on our way to its fulfilment.

Let me see if this helps you. My personal business card is printed on both sides. One side carries my name and contact details just as you'd think it should. The other side has a quotation from the yogic sage Patanjali printed on it. It surprises and delights people when I give it to them.

This is what it says:

"When you are inspired by some great purpose, some extraordinary project, all of your thoughts break their bonds: your mind transcends limitations, your consciousness expands in every direction, and you find yourself in a new, great and wonderful world. Dormant forces, faculties and talents become alive, and you discover yourself to be greater person by far than you ever dreamed yourself to be."

With that in mind take some time right now to formulate a want that is worthy of yourself and the SELF Service Universe. Once you have decided what you want write it down. Do it now.

_____

_____

_____

_____

If you have written it down then you are in the minority. If you have already got written goals for yourself stating what you want you are ahead of the crowd.

It might surprise you to learn that only about three out of every hundred people have written down defined goals they have set for themselves. These goals are a clear explanation of what they want. More importantly these written goals are a published statement to themselves (their SELF) and to the SELF Service Universe of what they intend as an outcome. No wonder it is these few who get what they do want in life whilst the majority do not.

As a happy, healthy and wealthy self-help author and mentor I know what I want and I use every edge I have to ensure that I get it. I am one of those three in a hundred and I am very grateful about that. Others are not so well placed.

So 97 out of every hundred do not have written goals. They must be relying on their mental faculties to keep what they want clear in their minds continually until they get it. Living as we do in these interesting times with all the distractions that's not likely to work for too many of them is it? Then there are all those negative thoughts, programmes and limiting beliefs to contend with. Well I think you get the idea. It is probably clear now why most of them inevitably get more of what they don't want, rather than what they do.

Now let us continue with our focus on what you want. If you did write it down before have a look at it now and consider whether you are happy with it. Have you, even in writing it down, limited yourself and the SSU through hidden negative thinking and limiting beliefs? Can what you say you want be bigger, better, more amazing? Well as far as the SELF Service Universe is concerned there are no limits but it is YOU who is deciding what to order. Why order a loaf of bread you can have the whole bakery? So re-write what you want again here but make it bigger, more ambitious and exciting.

_____

_____

_____

_____

_____

_____

_____

_____

Well done! The trick is to get over any sense of limitation. What you really want should be so big, so exciting that you will be ecstatic when it gets delivered. We will come back to what you have decided you want later when we finally put all the teaching and techniques together.

Now another thing for you to just be aware of is feeling guilty about your wanting. That is a very common programme although it is usually well concealed. There is no reason whatsoever for feeling guilty about wanting.

I have a very nice house. I am now deciding whether I want another home elsewhere. I could feel that I am being greedy or not appreciating what I already have. Neither would be true because I am not wanting from a point of greed and I love and appreciate my home. However I know that even after 25 years here it, like all things, is impermanent and I am not grasping or attached to it. As we know that is how we cause suffering for ourselves. So let us be absolutely clear about this: wanting is a powerful force for change when it comes from a genuine desire that is not contaminated with greed or lack of appreciation for what we already have.

In other words you can consider that wanting is a good thing as long as you don't charge it negatively from a sense of lack or guilt. I hope you understand this subtle point because in such subtleties negative thinking and limiting beliefs easily hide from your sight as they sabotage your dreams once again.

This is important for getting what you want from the SSU, so you should always have sense of havingness with regard to what is already yours and also to that which you have ordered from the SSU and are waiting for delivery. So right now I want you to stop and think about your life, your current circumstances and your possessions. Write down at least five things that you are really pleased to have in your life and can genuinely feel a sense of gratitude for.

_____

_____

_____

_____

_____

This havingness is a genuine sense of gratitude for the things, people and circumstances that come into, and out of, our lives every day. Even when things are not what you wanted, you should be grateful.

You might be taken aback at that. I am saying that your havingness must extend to the things that come along that you don't want. Why yes, absolutely! And I will explain why. You see things that you don't want are valuable too. Don't forget what I told you earlier about the truth depending upon your point of view. I also nicknamed this principle 'doing a one-eighty' didn't I? Yes, everything has the potential to assist you in your growth and journey towards that better life you want for your SELF. They are helping you become more aware of what you actually do want and are helping you fine-tune your SSU ordering skills as you go along. Don't forget that much of what you take for granted and do not appreciate could be someone else's treasure.

So if you haven't been in the habit of defining what you want and writing it down now would be a good time to start it as a beneficial lifelong habit. Remember what we have already discovered; if you always do what you've always done, you'll always get what you always got. If you are serious about changing your circumstances you have to change yourself and your habits. There are no shortcuts in getting reconnected to your true SELF and unleashing your personal power in the 4D universe.

I want to suggest to you that you get yourself a journal. This is a bound book of blank pages and it is a great tool for anyone who intends to get the best from life and the SSU. I have lovely journal that I call my 'feel good folio' and this is how I use it. I stick pictures of people I love and admire in it. There is a picture of His Holiness the Dalai Lama in there along with Sri Yukteswar Giri and Sri Paramahansa Yogananda.

You will also find Patrick Stewart as Captain Jean Luc Picard, Actor Robin Williams and Tom Baker as Doctor Who! Of course pictures of my children and my Grandson are in there too. I also use this 'feel good folio' to store poetry, inspirational sayings and pictures of my next dream car, home and so on. Whenever I have a few moments I open it at random and enjoy what is there in front of me. It is hard to remain negative when you have something like that on hand to lift your spirits.

I hope you get the idea and you can see the value of this simple tool. I will be so happy if you decide to make your very own 'feel good folio' and use it to keep yourself focussed and positive. If you do make your own do not forget that you have a VIP triple platinum unlimited account with the SELF Service Universe. So what is your shopping list of the things you really want going to look like?

WELCOME TO THE HOLODECK

Of all the beautiful truths pertaining to the soul which have been restored and brought to life in this age, none is more gladdening or fruitful of divine promise and confidence than this: that you are the master of your thought, the moulder of your character, and the maker and shaper of condition, environment and destiny. James Allen

So far we have explored how our brain is such an incredible tool. It is a biological computer, a quantum processor comprising billions of neuronal connections, accessing our entire bodymind through chemical and electrical signals and also interfacing with the SELF in the zero point field. It amazes me how anyone thinks such a marvel just 'evolved' but I'm not going to go into that now!

Your brain is your 'modem' to the SELF Service Universal allowing you to surf the web of unlimited possibilities. It is always 'online' and has the biggest and best broadband access too! As such it presents each and every one of us with unlimited potential. I don't know about you but I have a genuine sense of havingness with regard to my brain and its potentials.

We have also seen that, as your bodymind's hard drive, your brain can be your worst enemy when it is installing and running negative programmes. These programmes and also associated negative or limiting beliefs have been consistently adding wrong notes to the vibrations you have sent out to the SELF Service Universe. It is the overall negative or discordant vibration energy that has ensured that you kept getting what you didn't want. As long as your hard drive is allowed to run damaging programmes, limiting beliefs and negative thoughts it is causing you harm in your feelings and circumstances.

Don't ever forget that your brain is always 'online' and as such it is always transmitting something, some vibration, out into the SELF Service Universe and commanding the infallible Law of Attraction in your name. Even when you are not aware, it is still doing this. When you are asleep you are still transmitting loud and continuously to the universe. That is why you must cultivate strategies, like those I am providing, to develop and sustain a positive vibration.

If you go to bed at night with a mind that is running around in circles worrying about something you are not happy about you know what is going to be happening. You will be transmitting that worry to the order clerk at the SELF Service Universe!

If you go to bed feeling hurt, angry, sad or indulging in a sense of lack, then once again you are setting yourself up for more of the same. You know that your dominant thoughts and vibration become things.

This is very important for you to consider and for you to do something about it. When you are asleep 'you' are not involved with what your bodymind is getting up to. If you can't guarantee you'll manifest what you want when you awake, what chance do you have when you're asleep?

Well, I am going to show you that you don't have to carry on not having a chance. You can actually use your sleeping bodymind to help you get what you do want!

Using the simple but great power of meditation you can free your SELF, the true and eternal you, from the brain's software. I call this state 'detachment' and, if you have been diligently practising your meditation you probably know what that detachment feels like. It is through this detachment, this distancing of our awareness, our true consciousness, from our thinking, programmes and negative beliefs that we begin to see clearly what the problem is.

Of course by now you have also learned from this book the amazing little 'one eighty' trick of looking at things from the other way round. In doing such one-eighties you soon begin to notice something curious and yet very reassuring. Most of what you, and those around you, perceive as problems are actually opportunities in disguise! The very power and potential of your brain to install and run programmes is available for you to uninstall them instead. You can also choose to deliberately install helpful and positive little programmes.

By meditating and developing detachment you have identified some programmes and by not allowing them to capture your awareness and consciousness you are disabling them. You can install new beliefs and new habits simply by repeatedly thinking the new positive thoughts and by believing what you believe in a positive mode as opposed to a negative one. We have looked at how to change the vibration of our beliefs from negative to positive already. You need to actually do it and get them installed in your hard drive.

You have also had the opportunity to extend this detachment from meditation into your normal daily life as a quality of mindfulness. This is where you are exercising your awareness in all that you do as an overseer or observer of your thoughts, feelings and actions with the simple intent of keeping them all in harmony and positive in accordance with your goals.

Detachment and mindfulness are two powerful features of our brain and SELF working together for our good. But there is yet another amazing feature of your fabulous bodymind equipment at your disposal. It is the power of visualisation.

You can, and do talk to yourself mentally most of the time. But your mind and especially your imagination also use images. In fact your ability to create and use images is just as unlimited as any other brain potential. Inside your head you aren't just limited to creating and looking at a picture of something, you can create an entire and highly detailed 4D environment for it. You can create an environment that is, at the basic operational levels of your brain, indistinguishable from reality. Welcome to your very own personal Holodeck!

Most of us dream at some point during sleep and in our dreams we have a reality that is just as 'solid' as 'real' as anything we come across in our waking hours. Our brain is equipped to produce a fully equipped holographic environment complete with the entire necessary physical laws, lighting and colour palette to recreate any place or anything it chooses.

It is quite common for someone to have a dream that is just so real that it comes back to them during the day. In such dreams we are ourselves, just as we are in the real world, complete with body, mind, physical senses and feelings intact. In such lucid dreams we really get a glimpse of the incredible power of our imagination and our mental landscape.

If you touch something in a dream you can feel it. If you smell, hear or taste something in the dreamscape the effect it produces will correspond with how these senses operate in our waking state. How amazing is that? What is even more incredible is our dreaming ability to, when we choose, suspend or alter the physical laws of our waking life. Flying in dreams is a common phenomenon. Also our dreams allow us to be someone or something else that is very different to our normal life.

Such is the depth of detail and power of the illusion in our personal Holodeck that we can even actually experience a leakage of the mental holographic realm into reality from our dreamscape. This can be witnessed if you are a sleepwalker or have nightmares that throw your sheets off! So why is this ability to power up and use this limitless Holodeck of interest and importance to us with regard to getting what we want?

It is important because of something that science has discovered, tested and accepted for some time. You see the fact is that at any measurable level the bodymind cannot tell the difference between a mental simulation and reality. That is a powerful phenomenon that gives us a great asset in our need to control what we are commanding the Law of Attraction to do for us and to improve our personal wellness and happiness.

You have a built-in simulator on your Holodeck that allows to try out any skill, any situation, to have something you want, just as though it was real. Scientific research and monitoring of athletes, pilots and astronauts has shown that when they mentally simulate some manoeuvre or some complex act of physical co-ordination, their muscles and nervous systems react as though they were actually doing outside what they are practising inside!

What's more, they can simulate some task several times and then when they do it for real their performance reflects their 'practise'. It appears that all the observations prove that a focussed mental simulation might just as well be the real thing.

An American soldier was held prisoner for some years in solitary confinement. To keep up his morale and stay 'in shape' he spent several hours a day in his tiny cell playing golf on some of his favourite courses! He was simulating being on golf courses he knew well. He did this and kept his handicap up. When he was released he was thin and weak but he wasted no time in getting out on one of those golf courses. Can you guess what happened? Yes, even though he'd not held a real golf club in years he played the round to his handicap. You see in all of those mental rounds of golf that he'd 'played' in his cell he'd never bunkered a shot!

Now this shows just how real and how effective a deliberate and controlled use of visualisation can be. But remember the old one-eighty? If your bodymind cannot tell the difference between a positive experience of reality outside and a positive experience simulation inside, what about the negative version? Ah, I see you've realised where this is heading.

Recognise that your Holodeck, your immense power of visualisation is already in use a lot of the time in your daydreaming and your thinking. But is it under control? This is important because as we know at the level where it counts you, and the universe, cannot tell the difference between what you visualise on the inside and what you do on the outside. So if you are the habit of bearing a grudge, of playing over and over the scene of some bad situation, you are creating all the effects in your bodymind as though the replay was real. If you have daydreams that involve harming yourself or others then you are creating a 'reality' that is doing you no good.

I think you can also see that projecting into the future and using your Holodeck in imagination to act out some stressful situation you are not looking forward to is almost certainly going to deliver that stress when the time comes. If you must imagine something that hasn't taken place yet why not use the glorious power of the Holodeck to simulate a good and enjoyable outcome? You don't need to practise a stressful interview with the boss at your annual appraisal when you can just as easily rehearse your confidence and responses and so empower an enjoyable and successful one.

I hope you are following me in this because what you visualise and think about is just as real to the SELF Service Universe as the clothes you are wearing. Why replay bad things that have happened when you can pre-play great things that are yet to come?

When you have experienced a bad day or have experienced a negative situation don't abuse the gift of visualisation by continuing to experience it and its negative effects on your bodymind. Instead decide to play some nice music, relax and set your Holodeck to create some lovely place or situation that makes you feel good. Just think about this. If you could go anywhere in the world right now to relax and be happy, where would it be? Well you CAN go there, right now, without the cost or hassle of travelling courtesy of your wonderful visualising brain.

I have place that I used to go in reality many years ago. When I needed to relax and have some peace and quiet I used to go and sit on the top of a cliff in North Wales overlooking the sea. I especially used to love sitting there late at night in the moonlight. It used to do me a world of good and recharge my batteries as it were. Well it has been many years since I actually sat on that cliff top in Wales but I often sit in exactly that spot inside my Holodeck. The effect is the same!

So no matter how bad your day has been you don't want to make things worse by going to bed at night with negative thoughts and feelings. When you fall asleep your programmes will keep them going and your Holodeck dreamscape will keep the bad vibrations going. When I am asleep I want to know that I am still asking for the good things from the SELF Service Universe and not sabotaging what I had done during the day!

So at night meditate and still the bodymind until any stress or bad feelings have been put aside. Deliberately use your Holodeck to create something soothing and wonderful as you settle down to sleep. You can make the process easier by using sound. I love to fall asleep listening to the hauntingly beautiful and evocative music of Tim Wheater's flutes and Natalie's angelic voice. You can find out more about this wonderful mood music at www.timwheater.com. I think it would be a good investment, if you don't have it already, to get yourself a bedside alarm that can play CDs and has a sleep timer function. I love to wake up to beautiful music too.

One very powerful way to use your ability to visualise is to use it to support your positive feelings of having what you want. Remember the simple steps of using the Law of Attraction to get what you want from the SELF Service Universe? Decide what you want, ask for it, believe it is yours already and then receive it.

Well you can certainly use your Holodeck to explore and firm up what you really want. You can try out variations of things and circumstances (always in the positive way) until you have the goal you feel is absolutely right for you. Want a larger, better home? Well what will it be like? How many rooms will it have? What style of building do you want? Where do you want it to located?

You can experiment and explore such things inside your head with the power simulations of your Holodeck until you have it just right. Then you can ask for it holding the images in mind as you describe it to the SSU. Then you believe it is yours already while the universe starts making it happen. It s easier to believe it's yours before you receive it if you have a good, positive feeling of havingness about it and visualising helps this.

So the power of visualisation is immense and it, like all power, is a force for good or bad. In itself there is nothing intrinsically good or bad about your own personal Holodeck. It is simply a matter of how you use it that decides the vibration you create. Good vibrations are best, make it so!

PUTTING IT ALL TOGETHER AT THE CHECKOUT

There is nothing noble in being superior to others. True nobility lies in being superior to your former self. Ancient Indian Proverb

Well here we are at last dear readers. This is the final chapter and, in a whirlwind tour, I am going to condense the key teachings of the entire book down into this one chapter as a refresher course and to give you the formula for getting the best from the SELF Service Universe. This is not an easy task but I know I am up to it and so are you.

This chapter can only work for you if you have read and understood the far greater depth and detail explored in each page and chapter of this entire work. So if you find yourself lost at any point go back and find the detail in the book and refresh your memory. Then you can come back here and carry on.

The SELF Service Universe is standing by in readiness to receive and process your orders. You should have arrived here with a shopping list at the ready. At long last you should be totally sure and clear about what you do want. If you have done the work you have arrived here with a list of written goals. In so doing you have already elevated yourself to the top 3 percent of humanity and vastly improved your potentials for increased wealth, health and happiness.

So what we are going to do in this final chapter is to put everything we have learned and explored together. This is where we put the finishing touches to our understanding. The whole aim of this book from the first page right through to here has been to help you have a happier, healthier and wealthier life in future.

Your motivation to take this journey with me has been a sense of dissatisfaction with the way that your life has been manifesting so far. You wanted to stop getting what you don't want and start getting what you do want. This meant you had to accept that there were some important things you didn't know about the true nature of your bodymind, your universe and your eternal SELF. Things that, once explained and understood, would help you see how thoughts make things and what factors affect your thinking at the conscious and subconscious levels.

The journey has required you to see that if you always do what you have always done, you will always get what you always got. It is no good moaning about circumstances that you are unhappy about or do not want in your life. Instead you have to take steps to change your circumstances. To change your circumstances you must change yourself, your attitudes, your thinking and your relationship with the SELF Service Universe.

The SELF Service Universe is a sea of energy and consciousness at the quantum level from which all potential particles originate. This zero point field is the source and the foundation of all the dimensions and of all matter and energy in this 4D physical universe. Within this field of limitless possibilities is the sum total of all consciousness from all sentient beings throughout space and time. This is the home of our eternal Spiritually Existing Love Form (SELF) that has extended itself into the 4D physical realm as our bodymind.

We are not a body with an energy field we are an energy field with a body. It is this intimate connection with the quantum energy field that guarantees our eternal nature and provides our power to utilise the potentials awaiting collapse of their wave function. In this manner our dominant thoughts can and do become things and circumstances.

We operate in an interdependent reality where nothing is separate. All things are connected, specifically at the quantum level. Our lives unfold continually in relation to cause and effect, which is called karma. Every thing we do or do not do is a cause that will have an effect. There are no time-outs or free rides that will allow us to escape karma.

The law of attraction that causes the quantum field, the SELF Service Universe, to create what we intend is impersonal and impartial. It responds to the dominant thoughts whether they are good or bad. We have been absorbing negative programmes all our lives. Many have been implanted by external 'authorities' such as our parents, teachers, religion, politics and government. These negative thoughts, unchecked, will sabotage our wishes and intentions. We also have beliefs that can be very powerful influences in our lives. Many beliefs can be limiting and have a negative effect on our wishes and intentions.

We need to still our bodymind so that we can, as prescribed by Buddha, become aware of the illusions that cause us suffering. Our bodymind's grasping at external and impermanent things is a cause of human suffering. The method for stilling the bodymind is through practising meditation.

Meditation allows us to develop our status as witness or observer of the bodymind. In this state we become aware that we are not our mind. We can observe how thoughts and ideas spontaneously arise and fall. Through meditative detachment we learn to identify our negative thoughts and programmes. Once they are identified and we have developed immunity to their effects we can begin to dismantle these programmes and strengthen the positive aspects of our mental activity.

We also develop the quality of mindfulness, which allows us to construct and empower coherent thoughts and intentions without the distractions of mental chatter, and negative self-talk that had previously arisen.

Our brains have billions and billions of neuronal connections that provide us with virtually unlimited data processing, storage and retrieval potentials. The power of our brains is unlimited but we only use the tiniest bit of this, which is a great pity and waste. People like Leonardo Da Vinci who were multi-skilled in a wide range of disciplines and sciences were using more of their brain's potential but still only scratching the surface of what could be possible. We should exercise our mental faculties and think the unthinkable to stretch our range of thought.

We need to develop the ability of decision-making. Most people who make decisions are very slow to make a decision and then very quick to change or discard it. There are also those who make decisions very quickly and then are very slow, if ever, to change or discard them. The latter are the most successful people.

If you are not making decisions and thinking dominantly to consistently move towards your goals you are moving away from them. If we are not actively engaged in creating a better life we are disintegrating it.

We have beliefs that can be a powerful and positive support to us in our life but more often they are of the negative kind. We have seen how important it for us to honestly examine our internal belief systems and identify just what it is we do believe. If we have a negative belief identified we can do a 'one-eighty' and look at it from the other point of view. In this way we can retain the essence of the belief but reframe it in a positive manner. Having positive belief gives us power to reinforce our intent and give clearer orders to the SELF Service Universe. It is better to operate from true knowing rather than belief. But until we have removed our programmes and developed detachment and mindfulness, knowing is not reliable and so positive belief will help us.

Our physical bodymind vehicle is very important, as it is how our SELF moves around and experiences this 4D universe.

You and all humans are an energy field that has a body rather than a body that has an energy field. As such we manifest our bodymind from the atomic scale upwards. Everything in the universe from the smallest particle to the largest galaxies are simply an effect of organised energy. Thoughts are energy too.

The structures of our physical form have evolved in response to naturally present energy fields of the planet over millions of years. However modern civilisations have developed so much technology and man made power systems that the planet is enveloped in an electromagnetic fog. This is not doing us, our planet and all other life on earth any favours. As a result our efficiency as biological life forms is compromised and the basic level of wellness in humanity is below what it should be.

Wellness is more than an absence of disease and illness. It is our responsibility to find out what kind of shape our bodymind is in and to do whatever is necessary to improve our wellness through sensible nutrition, exercise and protecting ourselves from the damaging environmental factors.

Wanting is a good thing as long as you don't charge it negatively from a sense of lack. This important so you should always have sense of havingness with regard to what is already yours and also to that which you have ordered from the SSU and are waiting for delivery. This havingness is a genuine sense of gratitude for the things, people and circumstances that come into, and out of, our lives every day.

Even when things are not what you wanted be grateful. They are helping you become more aware of what you actually do want and are helping you fine-tune your SSU ordering skills as you go along. Don't forget that much of what you take for granted and do not appreciate could be someone else's treasure.

It is important to put our main wants down in writing as goals. In doing so we need to be sure we are not limiting ourselves through negative thoughts, programmes and beliefs. We should be sure that the goals are worthy of us and of the limitless resources of the SELF Service Universe. A goal should appeal to our hearts and minds and inspire and motivate us. The most powerful goal is the one that is so big, so amazing and so extraordinary that its realisation will change our lives forever.

By having written goals that we regularly review and update as they are realised we put ourselves in the 3 percent of humans that bother to do this. The other 97 percent have to learn to join us and therefore stop getting what they don't want and start getting what they do want. Their failure to develop clear, worthy and written goals demonstrates that they do not really know what they want.

We have an amazing ability to imagine, to visualise anything in our personal brain-based Holodeck. The illusion we can create inside our heads is as real as anything outside. In fact it is known that our brain cannot tell the difference between something we imagine and something real. The effects of a visualised situation will create the same effects in the bodymind as the real situation itself. We can use this power to maintain a positive attitude and instead of replaying bad experiences we can pre-play good ones!

Wow! I hope you found that whirlwind tour of the key points as interesting, exciting and motivating as I did. Now we are ready. It is time to place our order with The SELF Service Universe. Remember your biggest, best goal you developed earlier? Well you need it to hand now so we can get you on your way to a better happier life.

Placing your order with the SELF Service Universe is a very simple and powerful process as follows:

1. **Decide** what you want.
2. **Ask** for what you want.
3. **Believe/Know** that it is yours already.
4. **Receive** it with gratitude.

Let's examine this simple process and apply what we have learned on our journey here. That is the way to maximise the power and effectiveness of you ordering from the SELF Service Universe. It will also finally make clear to why I wrote the book the way I did and insisted on introducing and explaining everything we covered.

DECIDE WHAT YOU WANT

Well we spent an entire chapter discussing this subject. You know that very few people take the time to formulate meaningful goals or to write them down. Writing down what you want and fine-tuning your goals to be as positive and as meaningful as you can is a wise investment of time and effort. Most people are far more experienced at knowing what they do not want than they are at knowing what they do want. To attract what you want you must know what it is. Use you mind and heart to choose things that feel good and sound good. Enlist your power of visualisation for added effect. Remember to set goals that are worthy of you. Goals that are so big, so exciting and so magnificent that realising them will change your life and circumstances.

ASK FOR WHAT YOU WANT

The important thing as you already know from this book is that you must know what you want. That is what you need to focus on. Don't pay any attention to what you don't want. That kind of stuff is going to stop being delivered from now on anyway.

When commanding the SELF Service Universe ask for what you want with a positive mental attitude. Place your order with the confidence that you are fully entitled to do so. Don't have any doubts about the fact that you really DO want what you are asking for and that you fully expect it to be delivered!

Read out your order with confidence as though making a wish to a genie, guardian angel or whatever image works best for you. Don't neglect your very own brain-based Holodeck. Put it to good use by visualising your goal, the things you are asking for. Hold those images as you place your order.

It is good for you to talk to the SSU like it is this vast and powerful being come to grant your wishes. Actually that's not too far from the truth!

You need to ask with mindfulness. That means that as you speak your command your thought is exactly the same, word for word. Be sure to also have a positive feeling about what you are asking for. You know that this will prevent your positive wishing being damaged by negative thinking.

Ask knowing that the SELF Service Universe is on duty 24 hours every single day of your life to take your orders and to work on producing them. You can't catch it off guard and it is never too busy to pay attention to you. It exists for the purpose of awaiting your instructions and carrying them out. Your wish is the Universe's command.

You must place your order with a genuine air of havingness as we have discussed. Craft your goals to be worded simply and clearly in positive terms. Make them big enough and exciting enough to appeal to your heart and mind and so extraordinary that when they are achieved it will change your life. You don't have to settle for any less than the very best that you can imagine for yourself.

BELIEVE/KNOW THAT IT IS YOURS ALREADY

Once you have asked it is important to know that it is yours and then *let it go*. The first time you use the SSU to ask for something you will most likely have to believe. But once you get what you ordered you will *know* the law of attraction works.

You've asked for what you want so know that it is yours already and get on with your life. If you think about your order from time to time do so with a positive attitude of knowing it is yours already, it has your name on it. The SSU is a law-abiding service that is not going to give your order to anyone else. The moment you asked it had your name written all over it and it is being dealt with.

Just think how you'd feel if you were the order clerk in a company who had taken an order and put it into progress on behalf of a customer. You've done your bit with all due care and attention and you are trying to get on with things but the customer keeps ringing you and checking you've got the order. No matter how many times you tell him it is on its way he just keeps ringing up with the same question. Is the customer helping his cause?

So once you have asked for what you want that's it. It is done and there's nothing to be gained from checking up on it. Let it go and trust that it is being handled superbly by the universe.

Be careful not to start limiting the SELF Service Universe in any way by trying to work out *how* it is handling your order or how it is going to make it happen. You really do not need to know or bother yourself about the details! It is human nature and also a trick of limiting beliefs and negative mental programmes to start making you doubt. But it is okay, the universe is going to find a way to deliver what you asked for and you can count on that.

If after a while you don't see any sign of what you want you can begin to feel frustrated. This is a negative emotion and if I have taught one useful thing in this whole book it is the danger of negative energy. I know I have taught you much more but you understand my point.

If you start doubting shake it off *immediately* and adopt a positive mental attitude of knowing, what you want is already yours and on its way. You need to have a feeling of happiness like a child who knows the presents are already in the house waiting to be opened on that special day. A child has a magical trust and excited expectancy about such things and this is a great lesson. A child says what it wants for its present and doesn't worry about how or when mummy or daddy is going to make it appear. The child trusts it'll be there to open on the day. It doesn't bother about cost either! Nor should you.

You see the SELF Service Universe doesn't have any limits to how it can rearrange itself and everything within it to make someone's dreams come true. Neither does the universe have any problems financing even the most extraordinary things and circumstances for its customers.

Just because YOU can't see how what you wanted is making its way towards you doesn't mean that it isn't!

Avoiding doubt is crucial and why I spent so much time and energy teaching you ways to recognise and disable your sabotaging negative thinking. Have faith in your worth to receive and the SELF Service Universe's ability to produce.

RECEIVE WITH GRATITUDE

Somehow the SELF Service Universe is going to deliver your order. We really do not need to bother ourselves as to how. What is important is that you maintain your awareness and look out for the signs and clues from the SSU that it is rearranging things and circumstances in order to obey your command.

It is no good the universe attempting to deliver what you asked for if you are not ready and willing to receive it!

Sometimes a really magnificent goal will be broken into stages by the SSU and delivered in parts that come together. By having a positive mental attitude and feeling a joyful sense of havingness we are open to the signals from the SELF Service Universe that tell us where to look for our order as it is being delivered. It really doesn't matter whether it is a single delivery or several if you are receptive to the signs and clues the SSU gives you.

The SELF Service Universe will often enlist the services of other like-minded positive people who it will bring into our lives. When someone has something you need they will appear. Be open to all the possibilities. Many of the things I wanted and asked for came from unexpected meetings with people who played a key role in seeing that I got my order delivered.

I also know the SSU has used me in a similar way on behalf of others too and that is a great honour and privilege. In a way that is what it has done by having me write this book for you!

So look out for the signs and be ready to receive. While you are waiting the key is to feel the happiness of already having it. Cultivate havingness and use your Holodeck to visualise already having what you ordered. Feel how good it is that you got what you wanted! This is a very powerful tool that assists you and your wish granting SSU, genie, higher spirit, guardian angel or whatever you consider it to be.

When the moment arrives and you do receive what you want I am sure you will have no difficulty in feeling a genuine sense of gratitude. But it is always good to say than you. Thank your SELF Service Universe for fulfilling your order and enjoy it!

LAST WORDS

Well we made it didn't we? That is it dear reader we have reached the end of this particular book. I am so grateful that you have made this journey with me. I know that you will keep working to improve your skills.

What follows after these last words is useful information that can further assist and inform you. Please remember that my way is not the only way it is simply a way that works. If you have felt that my book has been useful then I hope that you will share it with someone, and recommend it to friends.

Now you have been introduced to the SELF Service Universe and the incredible fact that you are an eternal Spiritually Existing Love Form I hope you will continue to explore the possibilities. Reconnecting to your SELF by identifying the negative thinking, programmes and limiting beliefs and disabling them unleashes your true personal power and unlimited human potential.

If this voyage has helped you to understand that you can do and be anything you decide then I will consider all the hard work more than justified. You know that if you always do what you have always done, you will always get what you always got. That tells you quite clearly the simple secret to making your life better. You simply have to decide to change.

It is no good complaining about your circumstances if you don't like them. To change your circumstances requires you to change your thinking and yourself. That much should now be clear and you can pass this and the other simple but powerful truths and techniques on to people you care about.

If you keep getting what you don't want you now know that it is only matter of applying yourself to the principles and learning to express what you DO want. Enjoy learning and exploring some of the limitless possibilities of this SELF Service Universe.

There are so many wonderful and exciting teachers waiting to help you continue this exciting adventure. How wonderful is that! So please have a look at some of the details I have provided in the appendix and start investing in improving your understanding and skills for successful, joyful living.

Once again I give you my heartfelt thanks for time, attention and company. Also you have my gratitude for buying, using and recommending this book.

I'm Sheridan King. Thank you!

STOP PRESS!

In the very near future I will be publishing a book that deals exclusively with the spiritual teachings and wisdom as it relates to the Spiritually Existing Love Form. I will be writing this from my role as the Master Light Warrior known as 'Wandering Star'. This book is being published for those who genuinely understand the damage that has been done to themselves, all sentient beings and the planet. These are the ones I call the 'Light Warriors' and they are folks who want to be of service to all sentient beings.

The book will be a training manual and guide that will cover Master Light Warrior teaching techniques, the power and meaning of language, how to gain true spiritual power, special energy exercises, visualisation techniques, healing, and how to make a difference in a world gone mad.

It will be called "DO IT NOW! The Way of the Light Warrior".

If you would like to be informed when it is available then please let me know by sending me an e-mail to shez@well-wise.co.uk

SUGGESTED READING AND RESOURCES

FILM: "The Secret" DVD programme. This film has rapidly become a cult status programme showing you the power you have to get anything you want from the universe. The extended version is superb. The programme features success coaches, psychologists, scientists, doctors etc. including the truly amazing and irrepressible Bob Proctor, Joe Vitale, Jack Canfield, John Hagelin, Bill Harris and John Gray. You can view the film online or order it on DVD
For more information visit: www.thesecret.tv

BOOK: "The Field" by Lynne McTaggart, published by Harper Collins ISBN 0-7225-3764-6 A really interesting book exploring the Zero Point field and how quantum mechanics leads to the possibility that all things are connected. An extremely well researched investigation of a fascinating and timely subject.

BOOK: "Travelling free" by Mandy Evans. Published by Yes You Can Press. An explanation of how your beliefs create your reality and how you can change them.

BOOK: "The Attractor Factor" by Joe Vitale published by John Wiley & Sons ISBN 0-471-70604-3 The book that tells you 5 easy steps for creating wealth (or anything else) from the inside out. Also visit *www.attractorfactor.com*

BOOK: "You were born rich" by Bob Proctor available with other great materials from *www.bobproctor.com*

BOOK: "Ask and it is given" by Esther and Jerry Hicks with a foreward by Dr Wayne W Dyer. Published by Hay House. ISBN 1-4019-0459-9. This book presents the teachings of a non-physical entity (SELF) called Abraham. It is about learning to manifest your desires. It gives us 22 different powerful processes to achieve our goals.
See more information online at **www.abraham-hicks.com**

BOOK: Programming the Universe" by Seth Lloyd. Published by Jonathan Cape ISBN 9780224064385 A quantum computer scientist takes on the universe.

BOOK: "The Cosmic Ordering Service" by Barbel Mohr. Published by Hodder & Stoughton. ISBN 0-340-93332-1 The book that started the current 'Cosmic Ordering' trend. A guide to realising your dreams. Visit www.barbelmohr.de for more information.

BOOK: "Leadership wisdom from the monk who sold his Ferrari" by Robin S Sharma. Published by Hay House ISBN 1-4019-0546-3 This book introduces the 8 rituals of visionary leaders. It is presented as a modern fable and it's a captivating story that teaches and delights.
For more information visit; www.robinsharma.com

BOOK: "Cosmic Ordering Guide" by Stephen Richards. Published by Mirage Publishing ISBN 1 90257 824 4 A small but powerful book written in an easy conversational style. One of the many books dealing with Cosmic Ordering. The author is living proof of what is possible and gives guidance for 'achieving almost anything.'
For more information visit: www.cosmicordering.net

BOOK: "The Reconnection" by Dr Eric Pearl. Published by Hay House. ISBN 1-4019-0210-3. This is one of the best books on transpersonal healing and spirit medicine to be published in recent years. If you want to explore energetic healing – how your SELF can help you and others – then I recommend you read this!
For more information visit: www.thereconnection.com

BOOK: "Qigong for health and vitality" by Michael Tse. Published by Piatkus. ISBN 0-7499-1336-3. I met Michael Tse and his physical vitality is immediately apparent. This well illustrated book shows you how to increase your energy with simple self-healing techniques.

WEB: Wellness. To find out more about what wellness is, learn about good nutrition, obesity issues, weight loss, personal wellness coaching, natural beauty products and the various resources and business opportunities available, including wellness evaluations, visit: www.well-wise.co.uk and *www.teameuro.eu/sheridan*

BOOK: "Autobiography of a spiritually incorrect mystic" by OSHO. Published by St Martins Press. ISBN 0-312-25457-1 Osho (Sri Bagwan Rajneesh 1931-1990) is recognised as one of the 2oth century's most important and controversial spiritual guides and mystics.

BOOK: "Enlightenment: the only revolution" by OSHO. Publisher: Rebel Publishing House Pvt Ltd. ISBN 81-7261-070-X Discourses by Osho on the great mystic Ashtavakra..

BOOK: "Ancient Wisdom, Modern World" By His Holiness the Dalai Lama Published by Ababcus. ISBN 0-316-85863-3

BOOK: "The Dalai Lama's Book of Wisdom" By His Holiness the Dalai Lama. Published by Thorsons. ISBN 0-7225-3955-X The title says it all. Real and relevant wisdom from a great living Buddhist and one of the most compassionate men alive today.

BOOK: "The power of positive thinking" By Norman Vincent Peale. Published by Cedar Books. ISBN 0-7493-0715-3 A truly timeless classic for any student of how mental attitude shapes our lives.

BOOK: "Conversations with Yogananda" by Swami Kriyananda (J. Donald Walters) Published by Crystal Clarity.

BOOK: "The Monk who sold his Ferrari" by Robin Sharma Published by Element Books.
ISBN 0-00717-973-1 A great book with important leadership lessons, especially for anyone who has a senior role in business. Visit *www.robinsharma.com*

BOOK: "The saint, the Surfer and the CEO" *by Robin Sharma. Published by Hay House ISBN 1-4019-1163-3 Yet another great book by* *one of the world's premier thinkers on leadership, personal growth and life management. For more information visit www.robinsharma.com*

BOOK: "Star Ancestors" *Indian wisdomkeepers share the teachings of the extraterrestrials. By Nancy Red Star. Published by Destiny Books. ISBN 0-89281-819-0*

BOOK: "You can have what you want" *by Michael Neill. The Success Coach. Published by Hay House. ISBN 1-4019-1078-5 To find out more visit www.geniuscatalyst.com*

Printed in the United Kingdom
by Lightning Source UK Ltd.
118335UK00001B/82